A publication in

The NORC Series in Social Research

National Opinion Research Center

Norman M. Bradburn, Director

Social Science Information and Public Policy Making

*The Interaction Between
Bureaucratic Politics
and the Use
of Survey Data*

Robert F. Rich

━■◯━━━━■◯━◯━━━━◯■━

Foreword by
Kenneth Prewitt

Social Science Information and Public Policy Making

Jossey-Bass Publishers

San Francisco • Washington • London • 1981

SOCIAL SCIENCE INFORMATION AND PUBLIC POLICY MAKING
The Interaction Between Bureaucratic Politics and the Use of Survey Data
by Robert F. Rich

Copyright © 1981 by: Jossey-Bass Inc., Publishers
433 California Street
San Francisco, California 94104
&
Jossey-Bass Limited
28 Banner Street
London EC1Y 8QE

Library of Congress Cataloging in Publication Data

Rich, Robert F.
    Social science information and public policy making.

    (NORC series in social research)
    Bibliography: p. 193
    Includes index.
    1. Social sciences—Research—United States.
2. United States—Social policy. 3. Social surveys—
United States. 4. Bureaucracy—United States.
5. Policy sciences. I. Title. II. Series.
H62.5.U5R52   300'.723   79-92468
ISBN 0-87589-497-6   AACR2

Manufactured in the United States of America

JACKET DESIGN BY WILLI BAUM

FIRST EDITION

Code 8111

Foreword

□○□━━━━━━□○□○□━━━━━━□○□

During the past half century there has been a steady and in some respects spectacular improvement in the techniques of gathering social science information, especially sample survey data. These improvements in survey technology have been coupled with and to a degree caused by another major trend of the ·past half century. This is the growth of the "service delivery state" in which centralized bureaucracies design and deliver specialized social services to target populations of the society. In the United States, the social programs initiated by the New Deal legislation and then extended and augmented during Truman's Fair Deal and Johnson's Great Society have clearly established the responsibility of the federal government for the delivery of human services. But the policy makers and program officers in federal agencies frequently are in need of information about, for instance, the unemployed, the rural poor, non-English-speaking students, pregnant teenagers, and senior citizens. Survey research has proven itself a cost-effective technique for obtaining information about the characteristics and behaviors of target populations; and, to a lesser extent, for enhancing knowledge about the consequences of the social programs for the populations to whom they are delivered.

Thus, in the United States and elsewhere we have had the ability to produce detailed social science information coupled with the need for such information by government officials. Various labels describe this mutually beneficial linkage: social R&D evaluation research, policy advice, and so forth. Taken together, and largely funded by government contracts, these activities have become a major service industry.

It is inevitable that this industry would be subjected to investigation both by its own practitioners and by detached scholars. There are the beginnings of a research literature on the production and utilization of social science knowledge by the government. There has already been important commentary by skeptics. Many have felt that the social science community would be unable to produce information that met the demands of public policy makers. Academics could never meet a schedule or keep within a budget. The academic pace was too slow for the policy maker. Social science research, even if timely, would be too expensive. Besides, so the early critical commentary went, social scientists would refuse to or be unable to generate research findings that were sufficiently focused to be of relevance to the policy maker. Perhaps, wrote some of the early skeptics, if the social science community produced relevant and high-quality information on a schedule and within a budget established by government, then the supplier and the user of information would have grounds for a serious partnership.

Sooner than most skeptics thought possible, social scientists began to meet this challenge. Under prodding from contract specifications and procurement constraints, scholars within the social science community—often housed in special research institutions—have been able to turn the best techniques of social science to the questions posed by the policy community. The Continuous National Survey conducted by the National Opinion

Research Center was one of the boldest attempts to use survey research in the policy process. It failed. However, it did not fail for the standard reasons: Quality information was in fact produced on a timely basis. The reasons that it failed are the subject of the present study by Robert Rich, a study that forces us to think anew about the conditions which must be met if survey data are to be put to the service of the policy maker.

Rich reports that timely information of a high quality is a necessary but not a sufficient condition for the effective use of social science information by policy makers. Moreover, he reports, the sufficient condition is not under the control of the social scientists who procure the information. Nor is it a characteristic of the exchange between the suppliers and the users of social science knowledge. Rich argues that to explain the use, or nonuse, of social science information we must first understand its function within political and bureaucratic processes. According to Rich, the probability of information being used is less a consequence of the appropriateness of the information to the substantive policy than it is of the utility of the information to bureaucratic interests. There is, then, a "politics of information" that exists prior to the use of information for selecting among policy options.

A series of discrete findings make this larger point in Rich's study. For instance, he distinguishes between information as part of the problem-solving process (its role in policy making) and information as part of the bureaucratic political process, especially as it affects the career advancement of individual bureaucrats and more general maintenance needs of the bureau. He finds that use is enhanced if bureaucratic interests are enhanced. If the information is passed on to superiors by trusted aides, it is much more likely to be used than if passed on by less well-known aides. Indeed, the trustworthiness of the aide, more than the timeliness or the feasibility of the information, appears to determine use. Similarly, the form in which the information is passed through the bureaucracy is of more importance than the content of the information.

Rich also reports that "unique" information can be safely ignored, in part because no one else has it and thus it will not come back to confront you. If you will have to come to terms with the information sooner or later, it is better to appropriate it to your own bureaucratic needs as quickly as possible. But this principle holds only if the information will be widely distributed. Rich concludes that because process takes precedence over substance in determining utilization, social science information will be used only if it adheres to the protocols and conventions of the user agency.

In one respect, the central finding in Rich's book is reassuring. It is consistent with fifty years of research that demonstrates how social systems fail to work the way that preresearch commentators expect. Thus: Workers produce not because of working conditions but because they are paid attention to (Roethlisberger and Dickson); soldiers fight not because of patriotism but because of loyalty to fellow soldiers (Stouffer); consumers purchase not because of advertising but because of interpersonal validation (Katz and Lazarsfeld); citizens choose among party candidates not because of campaign literature but because of inherited party identifications (Berelson, Lazarsfeld, and McPhee; Campbell, Converse, Miller, and Stokes); people join voluntary associations not because of the goals of the organization but because of their membership in social networks (Sills). To these findings we add the argument in the present book: Policy makers accept information not because it gives focus to a given policy choice but because it sustains the interests of the agency or advances a career.

While we take away from this book the comfortable sense that sociological theory is again confirmed, we also take away two sobering reflections about the role of social science information in the policy process. First, though social science must continue to improve its technical and theoretical ability if it is to provide information relevant to intelligent policy making, factors external to the improvement of information production continue to substantially influence how successfully and creatively the social scientist can contribute to the policy process.

Second, Rich's book contributes significantly to our understanding of such issues as the incentives that lead government officials to use information, the coordination between the

production and utilization of information, and the difficulty encountered by government officials as they try to define policy
choices in terms amenable to social science research. These
issues are part of a larger theoretical puzzle—the role played by
information in governing complex industrial states. The present
era has been proclaimed "the age of information." Unfortu-
nately this proclamation has not been accompanied, as yet, by
a social scientific theory of information. As such a theory begins to emerge, it will owe much to the present study. But as
Rich would be the first to acknowledge, the production and
utilization of information in governing the United States has already, and dramatically, outstripped our theoretical understand-
ings. It is yet another illustration of how events and social
arrangements are moving more rapidly than our ability to comprehend them.

New York, New York   Kenneth Prewitt
August 1981   President, Social
                                             Science Research
                                             Council

To my loving parents:
Max and Adele Rich

Preface

This book originated as part of Donald T. Campbell's research project "Methods for the Experimenting Society." Campbell suggests that "the experimenting society will be one which will vigorously try out proposed solutions to recurrent problems, which will make hard-headed and multidimensional evaluations of the outcomes, and which will move on to try other alternatives when evaluation shows one reform to have been ineffective or harmful. We do not have such a society today."

In the history of modern United States bureaucracy, only a handful of true administrative experiments (experiments involving changes in organizational structure or operational procedure) have been funded and operated by public agencies at the federal level. From 1972 through 1974, the National Science Foundation, through its newly created Research Applied to National Needs division (RANN), funded several experiments to test procedures and mechanisms for the transfer of policy-relevant information to public officials responsible for decision making. In particular, RANN was interested in seeing whether social science data could be presented to public officials in a manner that would result in (1) the application of research results and (2) a change of attitude toward the social sciences as being more than marginally relevant to the concerns of government officials.

Social scientists have long believed that they can contribute to the pursuit of human welfare, but they also believe that empirically grounded knowledge is seriously underutilized in important policy decisions. Policy makers, on the other hand, feel that the reports they receive are unintelligible, do not deal with the immediate problems on their agenda, and are not sensitive to the unique pressures for action under which they must perform.

These accounts of the attitudes of policy makers and researchers toward their respective roles point to "gaps" in communication, common values, and common problem-solving orientations between the two groups. The contentions that result from these researcher/decision maker "gaps" are characterized by what C. P. Snow has described as the "two cultures" conflict. The notion of two essentially different cultures or worlds in which researchers and policy makers live encompasses some of the major problems to which federal officials must address themselves if they are to increase the overall utility of social research and development investments. It is often stated that a bridge must be built between the culture of science research and the culture of government administration. This "bridge" would result in overcoming communication blockages, differential priorities assigned to the quality of information, constraints resulting from the realities of the decision-making process, and differences between the bureaucratic and the academic reward and incentive systems.

The two cultures theme is at the heart of most studies of utilization. While best viewed as a "metaphor" rather than as a distinct social theory, it has been the central construct used to explain variations in the utilization and nonutilization of scientific knowledge. In the utilization literature, this gap is similarly related to some (or all) of the following factors: availability of information or data, relevance of the information, the form in which it is delivered, and its timeliness. When information is not in the proper form, delivered on time, or relevant, the assumption is that it will not be used. Conversely, it is assumed that if these conditions are appropriately met, then utilization will follow. In the broadest sense, then, knowledge utilization has been thought of as a problem of linkage—of building links between the knowledge production and knowledge utilization systems.

A competing hypothesis drawn from the literature on public administration and bureaucracy holds that utilization and nonutilization may be associated with institutional and bureaucratic arrangements that are quite different from factors traditionally considered important. According to this theory, levels of utilization may be best explained by examining routine bureaucratic or organizational roles and procedures: Are the officials who produce, disseminate, and use information following accepted agency practices? Are they sensitive to the ways in which policy makers are accustomed to using information? Bureaucratic rules, practices, and traditions may therefore be expressed in terms of formal and informal information policies that dictate how officials will produce, process, and apply information.

In this book, I argue that to understand the use of information in public policy making one must first understand the bureaucratic and political conditions under which public officials operate. The aims of my study were (1) to assess the extent to which one of the administrative experiments funded by RANN—the Continuous National Survey—was "successful," (2) to examine the extent to which the two cultures metaphor explains levels of utilization (as opposed to theories growing out of studies of organizations and bureaucracies), and (3) to analyze the uses that were made of the information generated through the Continuous National Survey experiment. Findings reveal that the success of the experiment, and the levels and types of utilization seen, are related more to standard bureaucratic rules and procedures than they are to factors such as timeliness, relevance, and quality of the data presented.

This work represents one of the first attempts to analyze

the knowledge production and use cycle (that is, the procurement, dissemination, and use or nonuse of the information). It traces how information is used from the time it enters the organization to the time when the decision is made to use or not use the data. As a result of such analysis, this work contributes to the theory of knowledge utilization and public policy making, as well as to our awareness of the effects of bureaucratic behavior on public problem-solving processes. As such, it will prove valuable to social scientists concerned with the application of their research to public policy making and researchers involved in measuring knowledge utilization. In addition, the findings will benefit public sector decision makers in federal and state government who want to increase the use of information and understand the obstacles that must first be overcome.

Acknowledgments

In completing this work, I am indebted to many individuals who have helped in critiquing it, reading it, and making suggestions for changes over the last several years. I had the support and advice of members of the Department of Political Science at the University of Chicago (where this study was first completed as a doctoral dissertation), faculty members of other universities, my family, and friends.

I am particularly grateful for the time and commitment given to this study by Gerhard Casper of the University of Chicago. He spent many hours reading and discussing various drafts of the manuscript with me. I also want to thank Kenneth Prewitt and James S. Coleman for their careful reading of several drafts; their advice, interest, and support proved to be invaluable.

Donald T. Campbell of the Maxwell School of Syracuse University lent financial, intellectual, and emotional support. Through his grant from the Russell Sage Foundation, "Methods of the Experimenting Society," I received funds for the many trips necessary to complete my research. During the early stages of the project, Campbell spent many hours with me going over the research design, refining it, and helping me to limit the study to manageable proportions. I also benefited from his advice on early drafts of the dissertation proposal and plans for data analysis. His excitement, support, and interest in my work helped me immeasurably, and he will always hold a special place in my intellectual life.

I thank J. David Greenstone and Lloyd Rudolph of the University of Chicago for their careful reading of early drafts of various chapters. E. W. Kelley of Cornell University and Kiyoshi Ikeda of the University of Hawaii were also kind enough to spend many hours with me discussing strategies of data analysis and methodological problems related to policy analysis. In the last stages of my work, I benefited from long discussions with Nathan Caplan of the University of Michigan. He was completing a study similar to mine at the time we first got to know each other, and his critique of parts of my central argument was very valuable.

I greatly appreciate my family and friends, who showed unlimited patience with my fidgeting and crankiness. My wife Lucy bore the special burdens of the frustrations and long hours that accompanied my research. Her great love, support, and patience made possible what sometimes seemed an impossible task. She also took on the thankless task of critiquing and proofreading the various drafts. Without her help, this book would not have been possible.

Princeton, New Jersey   Robert F. Rich
July 1981

Contents

5. Assessing the Survey Experiment   82

6. Utilization of the Survey Information   108

7. Future of Survey Research for Meeting National
    Needs   154

    Appendix A: Questionnaires   165

    Appendix B: Basic Coding Sheet and Summary
                Tables   174

    Appendix C: Agency Memos, I   182

    Appendix D: Agency Memos, II   187

    References   193

    Index   199

The Author

Robert F. Rich is assistant professor of politics and public affairs at Princeton University. He is a member of the faculty of
the Woodrow Wilson School of Public and International Affairs
and the Department of Politics. He received the B.A. degree in
government from Oberlin College (1971), the M.A. degree in
political science from the University of Chicago (1973), and the
Ph.D. degree in political science from the University of Chicago
(1975).

Rich was awarded several training and research fellow-
ships throughout his education, including a German government
fellowship to study at the Free University of Berlin in 1971. He
also received the American Political Science Association's
Leonard D. White Award for the best doctoral dissertation in
the area of public administration (1976) and the University of

Chicago's Mark Perry Galler Award for the best doctoral dissertation in the Graduate Social Science Division (1976).

Rich's main research activities have been in the areas of science policy, research and development management, the utilization of social science research information, and the dynamics of bureaucratic behavior. Most recently, he has been the principal investigator on projects researching the problem-solving models employed by public sector officials. His publications include *Government Information Management* (with E. Morss, 1980), *Translating Evaluation into Policy* (editor, 1979), and *The Knowledge Cycle* (editor, 1981). In addition, Rich serves as editor of the journal *KNOWLEDGE: Creation, Diffusion, Utilization,* which he founded in 1979.

Social Science Information and Public Policy Making

The Interaction Between
Bureaucratic Politics
and the Use
of Survey Data

As every man goes through life, he fills in a number of forms for the record, each containing a number of questions. . . . There are thus hundreds of little threads radiating from every man, and millions of threads in all. If these threads were suddenly to become visible, the whole sky would look like a spider's web, and if they materialized as rubber bands, buses, trams and even people would lose all ability to move, and the wind would be unable to carry torn-up newspapers or autumn leaves along the streets of the city. They are not visible, they are not material, but every man is constantly aware of their existence. . . . Each man, permanently aware of his own invisible threads, naturally develops a respect for the people who manipulate the threads.

Aleksandr Solzhenitsyn
The Cancer Ward

Confidence in the credibility of government can only be restored by a policy of making available to the fullest extent possible accurate and complete information on the nation's policies, programs, statistics, and other information that contributes to an informed citizenry.

House Committee on Government
Operations 1971

CHAPTER 1

Experiment
in the Application
of Survey Research

Few true administrative experiments funded and operated by a public agency at the federal level have been conducted in the United States' bureaucracy.* Especially rare are experiments designed to alter the day-to-day procedures and practices adhered to by one or more agencies. Certainly programs or procedures have been labeled as experimental or innovative (especially many of the Great Society programs of the 1960s), but very few such "experiments" adhere to the principles of experimental or quasi-experimental design. Such experimental "interfer-

---

*Campbell (1971a) differentiates administrative experiments from social experiments. Social experiments generally refer to programmatic "interventions" and movement toward change. Administrative experiments involve initiating changes in organizational structure or operating procedures; they may ultimately effect programmatic or policy changes.

ence" in the day-to-day operations of a busy agency is usually considered to be disruptive and unacceptable.

Yet in 1971 and 1972, the National Science Foundation (NSF), through its newly created Research Applied to National Needs Division (RANN), funded several administrative experiments to test procedures and mechanisms for transferring policy-relevant knowledge or information to public officials responsible for decision making. The experiments were to assess whether policy makers would accept particular knowledge-transfer mechanisms (that is, a set of organizational procedures) and whether they would use the information provided to them.

Officials in RANN who supported this program sought to provide federal agencies with new and unique sources of information, one of which was monthly and weekly public opinion or survey data. RANN funded an eighteen-month administrative experiment to test the feasibility of a multipurpose, multiagency national survey which would provide federal policy makers with public opinion surveys relevant to current issues. The objective of the survey was to improve the information base for the public policy and program decision-making processes. The success of this administrative experiment—the Continuous National Survey (CNS)—is the topic of the study reported in this volume.

Background

The adaptation of scientific knowledge to meet the needs of society is a recurring theme in western thought (Rich, 1979). Scientists, philosophers, and sociologists have argued that social change is directly related to changes in modes of knowing, changes in the way in which information is generated. Lynd drew attention to the importance of this phenomenon in *Knowledge for What?*, published in 1939. But, with the exception of studies carried out during World War II, the influence of the social sciences as a field and social scientists as experts was limited. The field developed as an autonomous social system and it continued as such with minimum regard for its social utility (see Caplan, 1980).

In the 1960s, the application of social science information concerned managers responsible for public policy programs and the allocation of research and development budgets. Blue-ribbon commissions (the Brim Commission, the President's Commission on Federal Statistics, the Commission on the Organization of Government for the Conduct of Foreign Policy) and special, new divisions of agencies (for example, the Office of the Special Assistant for Information) were created to address the problem of translating research into action. Most recently, the Office of the Science Advisor in the White House established the Intergovernmental Science, Engineering, and Technology Advisory Panel in response to state governments' desire to make use of the vast amount of research funded by federal dollars. The RANN program represented a commitment by the federal government to experiment with potentially feasible methods, knowledge-transfer mechanisms, and formal and informal administrative practices that would enhance the utility of social science knowledge for public policy makers.

The RANN program was, in part, a reaction to the role of research in the rise and demise of the Great Society programs. As Aaron (1978, p. 9) points out, during the Great Society years, "social scientists were actively engaged in the planning and later in the evaluation of programs of the Great Society." In the early years, one cannot be sure about the role that social scientists played in crafting, implementing, and evaluating the major social programs of the time. It is not clear whether prevailing social science knowledge was consistent with the ideology of the time. People believed in the programs being put forward, and their commitment to these beliefs was more important than rigorous forms of analysis. Indeed, as Aaron (1978, p. 159) points out, "This need, this passion, commanded analysts and others to suggest policies best calculated, given the available information, to achieve desired ends."

As it became clear that the Great Society and War on Poverty programs were not working, some officials blamed the social scientists who promised too much, too quickly; problems were not solved despite the promises that were made. Others reacted differently: "When the passion waned, partly because of external events and partly because of frustration at the apparently mixed results from national policies, the imperatives of the analytical process won out" (Aaron, 1978, p. 159). RANN was created in this atmosphere, in which it was uncertain as to what the status, prestige, and role of the applied social sciences should be. Moreover, it is important to remember that RANN was founded as part of the aftermath of the Special Commission on Social Sciences, which was established by the National Science Board in 1968. This commission, chaired by Orville Brim, "was charged with making recommendations for increasing the useful application of the social sciences in the solution of contemporary social problems" ("Knowledge into Action . . . ," 1969, p. xi).

The growing importance that was attributed to the social sciences should be placed in the context of the expansion of the knowledge industry after World War II. Between 1945 and 1965, research and development expenditures in America increased fifteenfold. Between 1964 and 1969 alone, the percentage of the gross national product devoted to research and development (R&D) increased from 3.4 percent to 9 percent, or by a greater percentage than any other country in the western world (Bell, 1974, pp. 250-251). Indeed, as Bell (1974, p. 212) points out, the U.S. had become a knowledge-oriented society: "The postindustrial society, it is clear, is a knowledge society in a double sense: first, the sources of innovation are increasingly derivative from research and development (and more directly, there is a new relation between science and technology because of the centrality of theoretical knowledge); second, the weight of the society—measured by a larger proportion of the gross national product and by a larger share of employment—is increasingly in the knowledge field."

In a recent study, the National Academy of Sciences (1977) reports that in fiscal year 1977, the federal government invested $2 billion to acquire and use knowledge of social problems. This sum probably reflects a major investment in the social sciences.

Moreover, regarding the translation of knowledge into action, figures compiled by the Office of Management and Budget (1976) indicate that many federal agencies are spending a large proportion of their R&D budgets on knowledge transfer and utilization. In particular, it is worth noting that the Department of Agriculture spent 46 percent of its R&D budget in fiscal year 1975 on knowledge transfer and utilization activities; the Law Enforcement Assistance Administration spent 13.6 percent; the National Institute of Education 10 percent. Clearly, agencies dealing with social science research are investing substantial resources to increase the utility of their R&D investments.

These budget figures indicate that government agencies are quite serious about translating research findings into action. The commitment is reflected in a requirement that contractors and grantees submit a plan outlining how their research results will be utilized with their request for research funds. It is also reflected in congressional appropriation hearings which, in the last ten to twelve years, have required cabinet and subcabinet members to document how publicly funded research results are being applied—What is the return on the taxpayers' investments? Several blue-ribbon commissions have been created to investigate the utility of basic and applied research in public problem-solving activities; most recently, the National Academy of Sciences (1977) sponsored a study on the federal investment in social research and development.

Rationale for CNS

In response to this growth of information and information-directed resources as well as pressure to make social science relevant, public policy makers felt that they needed to allocate substantial resources to develop techniques for increasing the utility of scientific knowledge. On what basis was this objective to be accomplished? What, if anything, had history or experience taught about the formulation and implementation of knowledge-transfer procedures?

Two Cultures Perspective. Despite the fact that the social sciences have been viewed as only marginally relevant to the concerns of government officials, social scientists themselves have long believed the application of their work to policy making would improve the quality of public decision making and, hence, improve the quality of life for the public at large. However, there has been some discrepancy in the perceptions of relevance; decision makers have not seen the immediate relevance of social science knowledge for their work and, consequently, both formal and informal interactions between policy makers and social scientists have not always been successful.

Among social scientists, the prevailing belief is that empirically grounded knowledge is seriously underutilized in important policy decisions: "Social science still accumulates in libraries and in impractical retrieval systems rather than policy and governmental practices" (Caplan and Rich, 1976, p. 1). Policy makers, however, feel that they cannot understand the reports they receive, that the reports do not deal with the immediate problems on their agenda, and that the reports are not sensitive to political and bureaucratic pressures. Decision makers are concerned with the restrictions imposed by the need for timely decisions; immediate partial information is more useful than complete information, which cannot be used, later.

Researchers and scientists feel that decision makers do not clearly communicate their needs, do not have a sense of how long it takes to produce accurate information, and do not respect research for the function it serves. Moreover, researchers' professional integrity requires that they not release information which is not of the highest quality.

These accounts of policy makers' and researchers' attitudes point to differences in communication, values, and problem-solving orientations among researchers and decision makers. These tensions are similar to those that Snow (1962) describes in discussing the humanities and the hard sciences as two separate cultures. Although most accounts of such tensions are based on the relationships between academic researchers and federal decision makers, they also characterize the relationships between researchers and decision makers inside government. (For a discussion of the significance of the "two cultures," see Caplan, 1979, and Dunn, 1980.) This notion of two different cultures encompasses the set of problems that federal officials must address if they are to increase the overall utility of social R&D investments. Specifically, this set includes problems of inadequate communication, concerns over quality of information, the nature of the decision-making process, the constraints that process places on utilization, and bureaucratic reward and incentive systems. These factors taken together are presumed—by the policy-making and research communities alike—to account for the limited use of social science information during the last three decades.

Communication Barriers and Blockages. Policy makers and research personnel (both in and out of government) tend to have distinct vocabularies and languages, which hinders the coordination of their work. A congressional study on the uses of social science research in federal domestic programs highlights the communication problems: Scientific jargon interferes with the application of potentially relevant findings. "The scientists' jargon acts as a deterrent to utilization. Complaints about the scientists' 'gobbledygook' come from every corner. This would also seem to be a symptom, rather than a cause. The language of science is a highly perfected shorthand for communication between scientists. It is effective for its purpose, but not for the purpose of communicating with the public or with most practitioners [decision makers].... What is needed is a special group of writers who can aptly translate research findings into language meaningful to the public and to persons responsible for their practical application"("Use of Social Research ...," 1967, p. 393).

In a similar vein, Moynihan (1973, p. 266) points to the potentially threatening quality of social science research from the perspective of public officials: "There is a ... general set of circumstances that contributes to the emerging threatening quality of the social sciences, and that is that they are getting complicated. The methodology of most social science is now quite beyond the comprehension of non-social scientists. In particular, it is beyond the ken of the lawyer class that tends to wield the levers of power in American government. Thus a priestly role of interpreting the mysteries is gradually emerging. And with it the anticlericalism of priest ridden societies. The simple fact is that it is harder and harder to know what it is social science says about anything."

The absence of a mutually understood set of terms (vocabulary) affects the ease with which policy makers are able to use research findings and research techniques; in addition, it adversely affects the esteem afforded researchers and research and tends to highlight the distinction between researchers and policy makers. Merton contends that levels of esteem and utilization are highly correlated: "Not only does utilization affect esteem, but esteem also affects utilization" ("Use of Social Research . . . ," 1967, p. 393).

The response reported by Moynihan, as a government advisor, and by the congressional study is one of some hostility and a certain feeling that the "two cultures" should remain separate, that some group should be responsible for mediation or translation. This problem is especially important when one realizes that policy makers want to make use of relevant information. Caplan and others (1975) report that 85 percent of the 204 federal executives studied believed that social science knowledge can contribute to the improvement of governmental policies; 87 percent agreed that government should make the fullest possible use of social science information. In other words, government officials feel they would and should make the best possible use of available data, but they need mechanisms and procedures to realize this desire.

Quality and Objectivity of Information. The quality, precision, and accuracy of information—its objectivity—also affect utilization. Caplan found that federal decision makers were concerned about the objectivity and accuracy of information; these individuals also believed that government officials did not have access to the highest-quality information. Caplan also demonstrates a direct connection between the quality of information and the use made of that information. In the cases in which policy makers consciously rejected social science information, he found that: "There appears to be no failure on the part of respondents to understand the meaning or relevance of their social science information to policy. . . . Information is most often rejected on grounds of objectivity. Objectivity becomes an issue when the data base is viewed as weak, the study design is poor, or if there is a general belief that there is so much bad research in the social sciences that valid findings are indiscernible, especially when two studies on the same subjects produce opposite findings" (Caplan and others, 1975, pp. 29-30).

Weiss (1977), too, found that quality was relevant in policy makers' determining whether to use policy-related information. Her study showed that policy makers are sophisticated consumers; they understand issues of quality control and make judgments concerning them.

Nature of the Policy Process. Lowering communication barriers and establishing objectivity are related to the problems involved in coming to an agreement concerning what policy goals should be and how policy is made. A clear understanding of policy is central to establishing and maintaining working relationships between researchers and policy makers. A State Department study concludes that the government has not received the kind of information it could use most efficiently because it has not been successful in communicating its needs: "the government only received abstract studies because of fundamental misperceptions which existed with respect to what U.S. policy was. Thus, no one felt that they understood what was required" (Einaudi, 1974, pp. 37-38).

Public officials are not in the practice of developing general principles that can be applied to many different problems; instead, their operations are focused on solving particular problems. A more general set of principles would be needed to dictate the development of long-term information gathering and processing capabilities.

The identification of specific information needs is dependent upon articulated goals, projections for future information needs, and projections identifying future problem areas. The nature of the policy process, which some scholars label a nonprocess, does not allow for this. A Presidential Commission on Federal Statistics highlighted this problem:

> The basic difficulty lies in defining the goals of a program. In the words of an official responsible for planning and evaluation in a government agency "when researchers say, tell us what you want" it appears that they are not aware that they

have asked the hardest—perhaps the impossible—
question of government. While it is hard to believe,
the government is simply not good at defining
what it wants to do in terms of needed social science research. It cannot meet the researcher's needs
for clearly defined tasks. Any proposal to improve
on the present state of affairs should recognize that
the government, in general, can only articulate the
area in which it needs information, as exemplified
in the request. Tell me something about mental
health. But it does not seem to be able to get much
below this, at least not on a broad front, to specify
questions which might have interesting answers,
and which might be answered by a single researcher
or small group of researchers working part-time.
The inability to specify the question to be answered,
that is, to specify the goals of a program, arises
from the fact that the issue of what the government should be seeking to do is basically ideological, not factual [*Federal Statistics* . . . , 1971, pp.
89-90].

Thus, the nature of the policy process and the philosophy of
the decision makers contribute equally to the tendency not to
collect or use information.

The consequences of these developments are important
when considered in conjunction with existing communication
barriers. Policy makers feel that social science knowledge is relevant to their work. They want to use it. More importantly, they
feel that they do not have access to high-quality information.
However, decision makers also cannot clearly communicate
their needs to researchers beyond the most general formula-
tions: "Tell me something about mental health." The reports
that they do receive are abstract, full of jargon, and seemingly
irrelevant to the operational needs of managers.

Nature of Incentives and Rewards. The realities of the
policy-making process serve to frustrate the public official responsible for problem-solving activities. They also, however,
reinforce the distrust and feelings of suspicion between the two
communities.

In addition, the reward systems within federal agencies are not oriented toward the use of social science knowledge. As a rule, bureaucrats and decision makers are hired on the basis of their expertise and knowledge in a given field. To a great extent their credibility, prestige, and legitimacy are related to the reliance of their superiors on their knowledge. As a result, many decision makers are reluctant to collect or contract for information from outside their agency or even from a different department within their own agency. Individual decision makers appear to feel more comfortable with familiar, traditional channels, whose value they can assess, than with an agency or individual with whom they have had little or no experience and therefore no basis upon which to judge the reliability of the information provided.

In this same context, Wilensky (1967) argues that the tendency to rely on expertise and not collect other information is established by the nature of decision making itself. Most federal decision making is constrained by considerations of time and cost. Decisions must be reached quickly and should be subject to the least possible risk. Given these constraints, Wilensky argues that the influence of established policies and interests will be greater than any other resource available to decision makers.

In referring to the reliance on channels of information that are known and trusted, one is implicitly considering all the factors discussed earlier: timeliness, comprehensibility, communication barriers, and an orientation toward the realities of the policy process. Thus, it is false to conclude that policy makers do not use social science knowledge; rather, they use the knowledge generated or disseminated by the social scientists within their own agency. One possible hazard of relying on a single channel of information is that an organization may report only those facts that support the position it wants the decision maker to adopt or the position which it perceives the organization has a stake in. George (1972, p. 777) depicts this situation: "In this variant of the workings of bureaucratic politics the other actors in effect 'gang up' on the chief executive and try to sell him the policy they have worked out among themselves."

Decision makers' reliance on familiar sources of information is analogous to their preference for familiar methodologies. Caplan and others (1975) report that decision makers consistently preferred studies that employed a distinctive methodology familiar to them and used those studies rather than those which employed a methodology with which they had little experience. Caplan's study showed that two methodologies account for the majority of his examples of utilization: program evaluation and surveys. The decision makers' preference for single sources or single methodologies definitely affects their decision to use or ignore information.

Competing Hypotheses

The two-cultures hypothesis is at the core of most studies of utilization and research results. It is the central idea used to explain levels of utilization and nonutilization of scientific knowledge. Proponents of the hypothesis assume that bridges need to be constructed to link the world of policy makers and that of researchers and analysts. The distance between the two worlds is related to some, or all, of the following factors: availability of information and data, relevance of the data, form in which the information is delivered, and timeliness of the delivery. Thus one hypothesis about the transfer of information is that if the information is unavailable, irrelevant, or untimely, it will not be used; conversely, if it is relevant, timely, and comprehensible, it will necessarily be used. (For further details of this argument, see Caplan and Rich, 1976.)

However, a competing hypothesis associates utilization and nonutilization with institutional and bureaucratic characteristics quite different from those which have traditionally been considered important. According to this theory, levels of utilization may be best explained by examining routine bureaucratic and organizational roles and procedures. Are the officials who produce, disseminate, and use information following accepted, legitimate agency practices? Are they aware of the ways in which policy makers are accustomed to using information? This set of rules, practices, and traditions may be expressed in terms of a formal or informal information policy that dictates how officials will produce, process, and apply information. (For further explication of such policy, see Caplan and Rich, 1976.)

Many agencies, as well as individual decision makers, appear to have an implicit or explicit policy (or philosophy) with respect to the use of information for policy decisions. This implicit or explicit philosophy governs how much information is collected, at what time and under what conditions information is collected, which types of information are of use to the decision makers, and what costs are incurred by the use of information. Information is only one of several resources which policy makers use in reaching a decision (Caplan and Rich, 1976).

If an explicit or implicit information policy exists, then it is directly related to the rewards and incentive systems in federal agencies. As already indicated, the expert has a definite bias against the information he has not produced himself, information he finds potentially threatening, and information which is not consistent with his values. As Rose (1973, p. 134) points out: "The more salient the information is to the core values of the policy maker, the greater his use for it. The greater the incongruence between the value connotations of information and the values of a policy maker, the less is his use for it." Satori also underlines the same point: "The stronger and more interconnected a policy maker's values, that is, the more ideological his outlook, then the less a man's mind is open to new sources of information. He does not need to be told more, because he knows deductively and as a matter of belief, all that he needs to know. The most structured intellectual outlook, that is, the most ideological, is likely to be that of the expert, whose professional training will make him predisposed to recognize some types of information and not others" (Rose, 1973, p. 134).

Given this analysis, it would seem logical to believe that on the basis of their training, experts will selectively collect and report information according to their intuition of what seems right and what seems wrong. This process represents a definite potential source of distortion affecting the use of information. There is a tendency on the part of decision makers to reject information that to them appears to be counterintuitive: "Many respondents who rejected policy-relevant information did so because they found the results to contradict what they considered to be true. For example, they are impressed by the concepts of democratic leadership and organizational management, and the data supporting these ideas, but given the nature and pressures of their situations, many upper-level officials were convinced that such approaches to management would be doomed to disaster. To illustrate further, although the evaluation of some governmental programs showed failure, program administrators and sponsors remained convinced that the programs had succeeded" (Caplan and others, 1975, p. 34).

Moreover, the organizational and bureaucratic literature teaches us that information—in the form of the expertise of an individual—is the foundation of a power base for any given bureaucracy. Formally, decision makers rely on their bureaus to provide all the necessary resources that are needed to solve a particular problem; bureaucratic interests are dependent upon the continued reliance of decision makers on these resources. This relationship leads, by its nature (both structurally and pragmatically), to the production of biased information and to the noncollection and nonprocessing of other information. (See *Northwestern Law Review,* 1974, for more details.)

As long as decision makers are relying on an individual's knowledge, there is little uncertainty in the transmission of information inputs; one would expect these inputs to be constrained by the articulated core values of the organization. The utilization of other channels of information involves the sizable uncertainties related to communication barriers between researchers and nonresearchers—two groups that have yet to develop a common vocabulary. As a result, only the policy makers who are technically trained generally make use of the available research based on these techniques. Other policy makers do not fully understand the capabilities offered by these techniques or the consequences which may result from their use. In a situation in which risks will not be taken unless they are calculable, information not related to the expert knowledge of an individual is not likely to be generated.

From this perspective, the principal purpose served by

knowledge utilization is not to provide objective fact gathering and analysis of high-quality, relevant information bearing on a substantive policy issue, but to reinforce the using agency's information policy and to maintain and strengthen the bureaucratic interests for control associated with the acquisition and processing of information in accord with that policy. Thus, information policy takes precedence over the substantive significance of the information in a determination of the contribution of scientific products to public policy formulation.

Caplan's (1977, p. 195) reflections on his earlier study support this perspective: "It does appear, however, that the major problems which hamper utilization are nontechnical. That is, the relatively low efficiency and low effectiveness of knowledge utilization is not so much the result of a slow flow of relevant and valid knowledge from knowledge producers to policy makers, but is due more to the fact that differences in values, ideology, and decision-making styles exist among policy makers and between knowledge-producer and knowledge-user communities. Thus, increased production of objective and policy-relevant data and further developments in knowledge storage and retrieval systems are unlikely to advance utilization unless accompanied by success in influencing the policy maker's understanding of the problems he faces, increasing his awareness of what he needs from research, and increasing his willingness to balance scientific and extrascientific considerations."

RANN's Decision to Fund a Survey

Given this base of knowledge, RANN was faced with the choice of adopting one of the competing sets of hypotheses, or trying to construct an experiment that reflected both bodies of knowledge. Leaders within RANN chose to subscribe to the implicit conclusions of the bulk of the sociology, communications, and information science literature; that is, that if the data are more timely, of high quality, relevant, in the proper form, and understandable, then utilization will follow regardless of the source—external or internal to the organization. This literature also points to the importance of a linker or translator to facilitate the match between the needs of policy makers and the realities of the research process. In other words, some official or researcher should assume the role of "broker" between the producers of information (usually researchers) and the potential users of the data or information.

Instead of accepting the prevailing beliefs, RANN could have turned to the lessons of bureaucratic and public administration theory. RANN officials might have taken the following position: Timeliness, relevancy, form, and costs (among other factors) do, of course, have some influence on whether information is used. However, these factors are subordinate to other barriers that impede utilization:

- the tendency of bureaucrats to defer to the expertise of colleagues
- the tendency to seek a monopoly of control over a particular information resource
- the tendency not to collect information from other agencies and from individuals or organizations outside of government
- the tendency to place a high value on sources of information that can be controlled, manipulated, and *trusted*

Accepted bureaucratic and organizational procedures help perpetuate the preoccupation of officials with issues of ownership and control. (Caplan and Rich, 1976, discuss these issues in detail.) Thus, according to these theories, which are formulated in the Weberian tradition, process takes precedence over substance in determining levels of utilization. This point of view suggests that one adopt strategies for change which are sensitive to the organization and bureaucratic imperatives, that one work with organizational reward systems; whereas the earlier hypothesis would lead one to formulate knowledge-transfer mechanisms and procedures. Obviously, these strategies need not be viewed as mutually exclusive.

In funding the Continuous National Survey (CNS) experiment, RANN accepted the former perspective. This perspective is consistent with the general RANN guidelines, which specify a need to: (1) provide information relevant to solving day-to-day problems facing decision makers; (2) provide this information in a form that can be easily understood by decision makers; (3) develop regular patterns of communication between decision makers and technicians, and begin to resolve the problems of communication between these groups; and (4) involve decision makers in information-gathering decisions so that they will have knowledge and confidence in the information they will be receiving. In other words, RANN was committed to "closing the gap" between the two cultures.

It was also consistent with RANN commitments to provide federal decision makers with unique sources of information. Prior to the CNS experiment, RANN thought that agencies could not use public opinion data in solving the day-to-day short-term problems facing policy makers because the process of gathering data (advertise a contract, read the proposals, negotiate a grant, receive a final report, and write recommendations to decision makers) required more time than was available for solving the problems under consideration.

Thus, RANN was interested in providing policy makers with relevant information that would be delivered on time, in a readable form. Moreover, the grantee would take on the role of the middleman, translating policy needs into researchable questions and research findings into reports in a form specified by the policy maker. Thus, experimental knowledge-transfer procedures would provide for an adequate test of the traditional assumptions made about underutilization: if the grantee could meet all of these conditions, utilization should automatically follow.

This commitment was also consistent with some of the major findings of the Brim Report ("Knowledge into Action . . . ," 1969, p. xii):

> Social scientists manifestly must be consulted in the collection of relevant information, and in evaluating social policies already in existence; their knowledge and informed intelligence should also be sought out before social programs are instituted. Even where they may not know how

to design substantially better programs than those
presently responsible for such programs, their professional knowledge enables them to detect and
avoid pitfalls in social program design—particularly
those pitfalls into which nontrained planners are
enticed by the charms of conventional wisdom. . . .

Although our concern is to increase the use
of existing knowledge, the commission fully recog-
nizes the importance to the nation of public and
private support for objective social research to provide a knowledge base in which applied insights in
policy formation can proceed. Even the present
utilization of knowledge and the insights of the social sciences is possible only because of the pro-
ceeding half century of such basic research. . . .

The major recommendations . . . , then, are
designed to increase and improve the nation's utilization of the strengths of the social sciences.

Given this background, RANN funded an eighteen-month
experiment. The National Opinion Research Center (NORC) at
the University of Chicago was to provide survey data to federal
domestic service agencies interested in receiving them. The data
were to be collected thirteen times a year and reported to the
relevant agencies every three to four weeks. The experiment
started in the fall of 1972 at a funding level of $983,400. At the
beginning of the experiment, four line agencies expressed interest
in participating in the experiment. (Details of the structure of
the experiment and the analysis plan are described in Chapter
Two.)

The success of the experiment depended on the fulfillment of the following conditions: (1) After the initial funding
period was over, the agencies would commit their own resources
for the purpose of continuing to receive the data provided
through the CNS; (2) the information would be used by policy
makers; and (3) policy makers' views of social science information would be positively influenced by this experience. In addition to these direct goals, the CNS experiment also had two implicit goals: To show that information gathering and use could

be coordinated on a multiagency basis, and to develop long-term quality-of-life measures that could be used the way social indicators are.

Having structured the quasi-experiment in this fashion, RANN was implicitly, if not intentionally, testing the competing hypotheses we described earlier. As illustrated in Figure 1,

Figure 1. Outcomes of the CNS Experiment

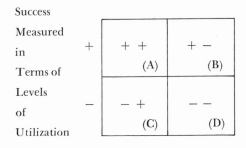

this complicated experiment has four possible outcomes. The analysis is focused both on the success of the knowledge-transfer mechanism—that is, a multiagency, multipurpose survey requiring cooperation and the sharing of resources—and success measured in terms of levels of utilization of the information generated by CNS. The data collected for this study will be used to assess which of the four possible outcomes seems most valid: (1) Cell A—the knowledge-transfer mechanism is invested in by the agencies beyond the period of the eighteen-month experiment and the information is used; (2) Cell B—the information is used, but agencies decide not to invest in this particular multipurpose, multiagency research instrument; (3) Cell C—the agencies decide to continue to invest in the CNS instrument, but have no use for the research results during the period covered by the experiment; and (4) Cell D—neither the knowledge-transfer mechanism nor the levels of utilization can be labeled as successful.

Figure 1 also depicts a clear concept of testing the competing hypotheses: the communication-sociology perspective versus the public administration and organizational theory perspective. Cells A and D best correspond to the traditional approach to explaining levels of knowledge utilization: levels of utilization are directly tied to the success of the knowledge-transfer mechanism. Cells B and C allow for alternative explanations—including the one advanced by those who adhere to the position of the organizational theorists.

Limits of This Study: Advancing the State of Knowledge

This study is limited by its nature as a case study: There is a limited data base to draw upon for reaching conclusions. Similarly, the approach limits the credibility that can be given to generalizations concerning the relationship between information handling and policy formulation, implementation, or evaluation. One could easily argue that the product of this experiment represents one kind of information that was being tested under a unique set of circumstances—funding from an outside agency. In the design of this study, these questions were addressed. The methodology (see Chapter Two) is designed to provide a broader picture of an agency's information processing activities than would be provided by a study of the CNS alone. Despite these limitations, the study is designed to advance our knowledge of how and why information is acquired, processed, and used in the federal government.

It is important to recognize that the social sciences possess very little systematic knowledge of how and why information that is designed from within federal agencies to be relevant to policy flows through them. On the aggregate level, something is known about how information solicited from outside contractors is used (Horowitz, 1967, 1971; Levine, 1972; Wilensky, 1967) and Caplan's (1975) recent study (funded by RANN) reveals how and why social science knowledge, as a whole, is used or ignored.

Something is also known about public access to information, and the success that individuals have had using the Freedom of Information Act. However, we know very little about organizational access to information. By *organizational access,* we mean sharing of information between agencies, sharing of information among subbureaus within an agency, and policy makers' access to information collected by the research personnel within their own agency. An understanding of organizational access may be critical to an analysis of the relationship between information handling and policy decisions. Public access looks at only one dimension of the problem: the relationship between the organization and those outside the organization.

On the organizational level, Caplan's research addresses questions of what percentage of bureaucratic officials use social science knowledge, what percentage of policy makers use social science knowledge, and what percentage of officials knowingly suppress information that could be relevant to a policy problem. Similar aggregate-level analysis can be applied to the kinds of social science knowledge that were used and to the general reasons for using it. These results were gleaned from general interviews with officials at various levels in the decision-making hierarchy.

This aggregate-level approach does not allow one to trace information as it flows through the decision-making hierarchy or to systematically analyze the criteria for selective use. We need to know whether other information was used instead and if social science information is unique in terms of whether or not it was used. Case studies allow one to begin to explore the complexities of the interrelationship between policy outcomes and organizational interests, personality conflict, externally and internally produced information, and the value given to expertise. This approach should allow for refinements of previous findings and the initiated new research.

This study seeks to integrate two disparate approaches to understanding the relationship between information resources and policy making. One approach focuses almost exclusively on factors related to the production of information and the other focuses almost exclusively on the factors related to utilization. There is a definite relationship between the two approaches that affects the formulation and implementation of information

policies. This study shows that the problem of providing relevant information to decision makers is not tied to quantity,
quality, or availability of information. Clearly, technological developments facilitate the production of vast quantities of information and rapid access to this information. Thus, we must
focus on the factors that influence how information is used.

The factors contributing to a decision to collect or utilize
information are complex and do not lend themselves easily to
causal analyses. However, this study documents patterns of
utilization and factors that influence utilization. It also com-
pares the CNS information to other social science knowledge
available to decision makers. This type of analysis enables us to
assess future possibilities for the development of experimental
knowledge-transfer mechanisms.

CHAPTER 2

Continuous National Survey: Structure and Analysis

The model for analysis developed for this study is based on the structure of the CNS experiment, the actors who were involved in administering the experiment, and the expectations of each of those actors.

Structure of the Experiment

When RANN was created in 1971, it was viewed within the federal government as the applied research branch of the National Science Foundation. One of its major functions, therefore, was to provide for the present technical needs of federal agencies and to anticipate future needs. Presumably, this office was placed within the National Science Foundation so it would encourage academic researchers to become involved with "applied issues," to anticipate issues that would be relevant in the future, and to provide knowledge about them—without competing with the responsibilities of line agencies. Because RANN was intended to fund applied research, all applicants for grants had to submit a utilization plan with their grant application; this utilization plan was to identify federal, state, and local officials who expressed an interest in the results of the proposed research.

To assess and provide for agency needs, RANN set up an advisory committee, the Federal Council on Science and Technology Advisory Board, composed of representatives from each federal agency willing to send a representative; the Office of Management and Budget (OMB) encouraged agencies to participate. In 1972, RANN concentrated its efforts on issues of concern to domestic service bureaucracies: the Department of Housing and Urban Development (HUD), the Department of Transportation (DOT), the Department of Agriculture (DOA), the Department of Labor (DOL), the Department of Interior (DOI), and the Department of Health, Education, and Welfare (HEW).

Working with the staff of RANN, the advisory board identified a major priority: providing for policy-relevant information that would be understandable and useful to decision makers. More specifically, the advisory board wanted to give agencies the opportunity to develop in-house information-gathering capabilities that would be seen as useful and effective by both policy makers and technicians within the agencies. One of the major in-house programs that the board wanted to encourage was the continuous collection of public opinion survey data. Public opinion data was obviously a resource of growing importance; policy makers and staff needed to become familiar with it.

To comply with RANN guidelines, potential users had to be identified before the grant for the survey could be awarded. Initially DOA, HUD, DOT, and HEW identified themselves as willing to participate. Some of the potential users sat on the advisory board and others were invited to become involved by the program manager at NSF.

Timing and Scheduling. As illustrated in Figure 2, the CNS experiment had several phases. Once the CNS experiment

Figure 2. Sequencing of Significant Events

The CNS

One year	Six months	Twelve months	No specified period
Phase I	Phase II	Phase III	Phase IV
RANN Identification of priorities and needs	Planning NORC meets with users	CNS operating Agencies receiving results	Agencies make decisions of whether to fund CNS

The CNS concept emerges	Preparation for "Going to the field" with specific questions	Agencies Evaluating the utility of the CNS	Potentially making use of CNS results
The experiment is funded			

was initiated (phase 1), three phases were projected: The first six months of the grant (phase 2) were to be devoted to planning—NORC and NSF would jointly identify additional potential users and decisions about operational methods (for example, the questions to be asked) would be reached during this period. The next twelve months (phase 3) would be devoted to the collection and reporting of the CNS—NORC would conduct thirteen surveys during this twelve-month period, and results would be reported to the participating agencies every three to four weeks. Finally, during phase 4, after the twelve months of field work, agencies were to decide whether to invest their own funds for continued participation in the survey. The span of this last phase was not specified by NSF.

Constraints Specific to the Grant. No constraints were

put on the agencies regarding the type of questions they could ask, the number of different agencies within their department that could be involved, or the way in which they used the time allocated to them for the thirteen cycles. The only constraint was the amount of time allocated to each agency for the thirteen cycles; each agency had to decide how to apportion its time among the interested participants within the agency.

It was the objective of the NSF that, as the survey developed over time, participants would learn to ask questions that were particularly well suited to survey research and to avoid ones that could more efficiently be studied by other data collection instruments. NSF and NORC also wanted top-level officials within cabinet departments to actively participate in the experiment.

NORC was expected to rectify all the conditions that were presumed to have impeded prior utilization of social science knowledge. They were to help agencies specify the questions they wanted to ask, translate these questions into survey research questions, and then provide the results of the research to the participants. The results were to be provided in the form of marginal frequency distributions—that is, so many people said X, and so many said Y. Agencies were to specify whether they wanted written interpretations or more sophisticated analysis.

The role of NSF after the initial planning period (phases 1 and 2) was not well specified. Would NSF, as a federal agency, continue to report its staff's wishes and interests to NORC or would it, as a research agency, give the grant and not interfere until the next report was prepared? This question was not resolved at the beginning of the project and was not understood by NORC or the participating agencies.

The Survey Instrument. Finally, we must consider the nature of the data collection instrument itself. The CNS was to be a multipurpose survey that could function for many different agencies.

Surveys are identified both in terms of their substance and their sponsor. In terms of substance, surveys may focus on a particular subject—whites' attitudes toward blacks—or a particular event—the election of 1976—or a series of unrelated subjects and issues. Similarly, surveys may be sponsored by a single source or by a variety of sources; the former is usual for surveys confined to one subject, the latter for surveys about a series of seemingly unrelated issues. A survey funded by a variety of sources is called an *amalgam.*

CNS was designed as an amalgam. The money allocated to NORC was based on the cost of a certain amount of survey time to be repeated thirteen times a year. Agencies were allocated specific shares of time; there were sufficient funds to allow for additional agencies if they became interested. The survey was conceived of as an amalgam both in terms of *substance* and *funding sources.* Once the grant period expired, interested agencies would contribute their own funds to the survey.

In addition to these basis parameters, interagency sharing of information resources was a feature of this survey. NORC was to collect all the background information on individual respondents to the survey—sex, race, education, income, and the like. The background information was to be reported with the frequency distributions for the specific questions requested by the individual agency participants. Moreover, agencies were not allowed to duplicate questions. If two or more agencies were interested in energy policy, for example, they had to work together and pool their available survey time. Finally, agencies did not have proprietary rights over the data—data could be shared upon request with the other agency participants and, after initial analyses were completed, with other researchers.

Model for Analysis

Utilization of knowledge is the product of the interactions of the actions of three parties in the knowledge-inquiry system: sponsors, information producers (researchers), and information users (decision makers). Thus we must examine the attitudes and behavior concerning utilization of sponsors, producers, and users. Each link in this system can influence the degree to which social science knowledge affects policy making and decision making. In the CNS project, another actor played a pivotal role: the Office of Management and Budget (OMB). Because all requests for information to be collected by a federal agency must be approved by the Statistical Policy Division of OMB, OMB can facilitate a data collection effort that it approves of or block one that appears to be inappropriate for federal investments.

The sponsor of applied research (either RANN or a federal service agency) can, potentially, play a critical role in the overall knowledge-inquiry system. A sponsor can be both the funder of research and the primary intermediary (middleman) in facilitating or promoting utilization. In that position sponsors can exert considerable influence on the degree to which research is used in policy making. Thus, it is not sufficient to examine the working relationships between researchers and users nor is it appropriate—given the role of a sponsor—to concentrate exclusively on the behavior of users.

A knowledge-inquiry system develops in four stages: funding, research, analysis and reporting of results, and summative evaluation. At each of these stages, the sponsors, researchers, users, and monitors play some role in influencing the ultimate outcome. Clearly, what occurs at one stage of development may have a significant effect on the next stage. One cannot analyze a particular phase of the knowledge-inquiry process without knowing what factors are impinging on the actors as a result of interactions during previous stages of development.

Thus, our model calls for the analysis of the behaviors and attitudes of the four major groups of actors at each of four developmental stages of the knowledge-inquiry system. An analysis of these data provides a representative picture of the explicit and implicit information policies of the participating agencies. To determine this overall policy, to the extent that it exists, three levels of analysis are appropriate: The relationship between the agencies' use of public opinion data (the CNS) and policy decisions; the relationship between uses of social science information, as a whole, and policy decisions; and the relationship between the use of information in general and policy decisions. Thus we can differentiate and compare the factors that determine use in general and the factors that influence the use of CNS data.

Essentially, this model tries to document types of behavior, on the part of any of the relevant actors, that would significantly alter the quasi-experimental conditions specified in the formulation of the CNS grant.

In making this assessment, we will focus on the following questions: Was the information requested by the agencies relevant to high-level policy making (concerns of the assistant secretary and above)? Was the assistant secretary's office consulted in the writing of the questions on the topics to be covered? Were the questions relevant to the problem-solving agendas of the top-level policy makers? We will answer these questions by comparing the expectations of the policy makers and those of the technicians concerning the use of the information, and by examining the questions asked on the CNS questionnaires.

We also need to determine the extent to which those responsible for policy formulation, evaluation, and implementation were attentive to the CNS experiment. We will consider (1) the level of the agency's decision-making hierarchy at which NORC entered; (2) whether NORC then worked with one person or bureau or with a larger or more diverse group within a department; (3) whether anyone responsible for high-level policy making met regularly with NORC; (4) the extent to which those responsible for policy decisions participated in the formulation of questions and analysis of results; and (5) whether those responsible for agency policy making viewed the CNS differently than the individuals assigned to work with NORC. These variables characterize an agency's organizational hierarchy and participation. For our analysis, we must determine if, for example, the objective of involving upper-level policy makers was achieved. If this was not achieved at any point in the experiment, then it is not realistic to use this as a criterion for the evaluation of success.

Similarly, we can examine the relationship between the researchers and users, and between the sponsor and OMB in the design of the experiment. We want to determine the extent to which sponsors and researchers were working toward the same objectives, were committed to the success of the experiment, and were agreed on the products and services that were to be delivered to the user. Our analysis should also focus on the goals that were set by the funding agency with respect to use. Since RANN wanted the information to be used for policy purposes, a measure of the experiment's success is the regular use of CNS information in policy making. Relationships between sponsors and users can be evaluated by analyzing the parties' agreement on goals, products, and services to be delivered. More importantly, we must ascertain whether both parties understood the role that each was to play in the development of the overall knowledge-inquiry system. In the ideal case, both parties share a mutually reinforcing set of expectations.

In analyzing the four phases of the CNS experiment, we need to consider any documented constraints. Such constraints affect our selection of criteria for success and our evaluation of whether the criteria were met. Having documented any overall constraints, we can analyze the success of the knowledge-transfer mechanism, with success measured in terms of types and levels of utilization.

As already indicated, this study analyzes each stage of the development of the knowledge-inquiry system. For each stage of development, a set of descriptive and analytical questions were formulated. The descriptive questions concern the number of participants from each agency and their place in the organizational hierarchy, the number of agencies and new participants added at each stage of development, the types of questions asked and how they changed over time, and the perception of the quality and utility of the information provided. We also document the participants' perceptions of success or failure at various stages of the experiment.

The analytical questions were framed to provide comparisons of the perceptions of various actors and the constraints that divergences in these perceptions placed on the project. The quality of use of the information produced and the criteria employed to evaluate the project—from the perspective of each actor—were also examined.

Data Base for Analysis. All actors involved with the CNS experiment were interviewed and related documentation was collected. The CNS experiment lasted twenty-four months—eighteen months of experimentation and six months after NSF funding expired. During that time, thirty-eight individuals were directly involved in providing the information (NORC), utilizing the information (the participating agencies), and providing the initial funding (NSF and RANN). Each of these participants was interviewed on at least one occasion during the twenty-four month period. Twenty-four of these individuals had only minimum contact with the CNS project. Some agency participants were involved with the project for only one or two cycles (each cycle represents a month; reports were provided for each cycle). Similarly, some NORC participants were involved with the project for only one or two cycles, and some NSF participants were involved in only one phase of the project. Individuals with minimal contact were interviewed on only one or two occasions. The fourteen more active participants were interviewed as long as they continued to have contact with the project, on five or six occasions. (See Appendix A for a full schedule of questions.) Four questionnaires were used to conduct these interviews: one for NORC participants, one for agency participants, one for OMB actors—because of the coordinating role that they assumed—and one for the NSF and RANN participants. The agency questionnaires covered ten general areas: (1) why the agency wanted to become involved in the project; (2) how the agency evaluated the success of the CNS experiment; (3) why the agency decided to continue or discontinue its participation in the experiment; (4) the agency's evaluation of NORC and the NORC personnel involved in the project; (5) how this project related to the agency's other information-gathering and analysis activities; (6) the manner in which the information was collected, analyzed, used, and evaluated in comparison to other information resources; (7) the use made of these kinds of data prior to the CNS experiment; (8) the specific use of CNS information: once the NORC report was received, who (within the agency) received it and what was done with it; (9) the utilization of other information resources in the same policy area to which the CNS information was being applied; and (10) the factors critical to the agency's decisions concerning how to use information. In each case, individual participants were asked to distinguish between the agency's evaluation and their own individual evaluations. Participants were also asked to indicate who (individual or group) was responsible for making the agency's evaluation.

The other questionnaires examined these same general areas, emphasizing the particular actor's role. The OMB questionnaire focused on coordination and clearance activities: What role did OMB participants see for themselves? How did they evaluate the agency's role in NORC's services? How did public opinion data relate to overall federal information policies? How was OMB able to use the information collected? OMB was also asked to identify any special or peculiar constraints that influenced the manner in which CNS information was utilized. In addition, OMB was asked to compare the use of the CNS to other information resources available to agencies in the same policy area. NORC's relationship with each participating agency during each phase of the experiment was examined: how successful did they think the experiment was, what were its strengths and weaknesses, and what would they do differently in the future? NSF and RANN were asked why they funded this experiment, how they chose the agencies to be involved, how they perceived their role after the experiment was funded, and what the future role of this kind of information resource would be. Each of the interviews was taped and transcribed; in only three cases did individuals request that conversations not be recorded. After an initial interview period they allowed taping of subsequent conversations.

In addition to these transcripts, all available written documentation related to the experiment was collected. This included NORC's notes on its meetings with agency participants, correspondence between NORC and other participants (NSF, OMB, and the agencies), copies of each of the questionnaires used in the field, copies of the written reports submitted to the agencies on the basis of the data collected by NORC, memos and reports written by members of an agency on the basis of the NORC reports, agency memos evaluating NORC's services, memos written by policy makers in response to memos written by their staff, and letters concerning the CNS experiment from participants in one agency to participants in another agency.

Written documentation that was not available in written form was either read or summarized during the taped interviews. Only one agency official felt it was inappropriate to show or summarize in-house memorandums.

These interviews yielded a representative picture of the information policies of these federal bureaucracies. Our analysis of this policy includes the decisions to collect and continue to receive the CNS information and the decisions concerning the utilization of this information. By tracing the flow of information, we can locate those places within the organizational hierarchy that are most critical to decision making.

Three levels of analysis are appropriate for the study of information policies and their effect on policy making: the relationship between an agency's use of public opinion data and its policy making; the relationship between the uses of social science information and policy making; and the relationship between the use of all information and policy making. In terms of the generalizability of this study, the third relationship is the most important.

General Analysis Plan. On the basis of the interviews and the analysis of information flows, we can assess the effect CNS information had, that is, the uses made of it in policy making. Establishing direct linkages between information resources and policy outcomes is, of course, difficult. Clearly, decision making is not a strictly causal process in which resources (inputs) and decisions (outputs) are directly related. However, our analysis of information flows enables us to assess the uses made of the CNS information. In addition, we can examine whether the use of information by decision makers is dependent on their level in the decision-making hierarchy and whether the use of information is restricted to particular forms (for example, summary memo, full report). Finally, we will determine whether various types of CNS information were used more than others. NORC collected and reported three kinds of information: general social and political attitudes, social inventory (possessions, consumption), and evaluations of ongoing programs. Our analysis of information flows will show whether policy makers systematically preferred any one kind of information.

The interview data and analysis of information flows will then be applied to the two other levels of analysis: the relationship between public opinion information and the overall information needs of a particular agency, and the relationship between an agency's information policy with respect to public opinion data and its overall information policy.

Methods of Analysis. Answering the questions central to this study required an analysis of the data collected, both in terms of its usefulness to particular decision makers and its place in the context of an agency's overall information policy. Confidentiality was pledged to all participants; therefore, no names of individual actors or agencies are used in the analysis.

From the interviews, we determined the kinds of uses made of the information requested and the patterns of transmitting information through the organizational hierarchy. We can distinguish seven categories of use: no use at all—information remained on the desk of the individual or bureau that received it; recipient made no use of it, but sent it to someone who used it; general background—but no other specific use; recipient wrote memos to superiors on the basis of the NORC data; recipient wrote memos to colleagues at the same level of the public decision-making hierarchy; recipient wrote reports for congressional presentations; recipient wrote a report for a meeting of the department's assistant secretaries and secretary; recipient sent the full NORC report to superiors. These categories combine ways of transmitting information with types and users.

In considering the uses made of this information, we must distinguish between *instrumental* use, of the kinds just described, and use which had a *conceptual* influence even though no direct output resulted. For example, although data were not used for policy purposes, their presence may have enabled policy personnel to recognize, for the first time, that such data are essential for the formulation of policy. In other words, personnel accept the usefulness of the methodology although they make no direct use of the data. With respect to the utilization of information, quantity of use is less important than quality or kind of use.

We then integrate the analysis of utilization with an analysis of the flow of information through the decision-making hierarchy. For each of the reports submitted by NORC, we documented the patterns of dissemination, the form in which the information was sent, and the patterns of selectivity—what information was filtered out. The range of descriptions of the form in which information was sent include such categories as "the staff member wrote an accurate summary of a NORC report" and "the staff member quoted parts of the NORC report in an inaccurate summary of the report." In analyzing selectivity, we assumed that some filtering of information is inevitable and useful; a report that provides a superfluity of information is not necessarily better than one that selectively summarizes information. Thus both the amount of filtering and the quality of filtering affect decision making.

Finally, we will make an assessment independent of the participants' perceptions of the CNS project. This assessment concerns the appropriateness of the participants' use of survey research methodology: the perspectives and expectations of NORC, RANN, and the agencies with respect to the information to be provided, the form of that information, the use of that information, and the effect it had on policy formulation. We will assess whether the judgments made by the individual actors were well founded by evaluating the extent to which the participants reached the intended goals of the experiment, actively worked on reaching these goals, and cooperated with one another in reaching these goals.

Definitions of Concepts and Measures

Before describing the details of the CNS project, we need to define several terms.

Information designates any materials (books, articles, statistics, and the existing literature) and data (surveys, evaluation studies, other contract research) collected by an individual or group. *Information* includes the following: recorded knowledge in the public domain as the existing literature, the history of a given event, public records, completed studies that have been committed to paper; recorded knowledge that is considered confidential and, therefore, exists only in the files, memos, reports, or telegrams of individuals or agencies; research contracted by an agency—including evaluation studies, surveys, and other contract research; in-house research; and research reports communicated orally. The critical property of this definition is that the information is collected—someone reads existing materials (familiar or unfamiliar to the reader), undertakes a new study, or orally communicates the material. Collecting information involves gathering and synthesizing materials that are not known to those requesting it; it is not, therefore, a passive activity. One either possesses information—within one's files, on the bookshelf, in the library—or needs to collect it.

Information, thus, can be distinguished from *expertise,* which refers to knowledge possessed by an individual in a particular area. *Expertise* also denotes the technical and methodological skills possessed by an individual. An individual may apply either form of expertise to solving a problem without having to collect any new material: knowledge can be recalled in the problem-solving process, and technical skills can be applied to establish methods for solving a particular problem. An expert may ask for information to be collected, but *expertise* denotes those skills that he or she applies to a problem without having acquired any new information. An expert's knowledge and skills may be of help in collecting new information; however, the act of collecting new information and the new information are not comprised in his or her expertise.

One of the main goals of the CNS experiment was to provide policy-relevant information. *Policy-relevant* refers to that information which the decision maker decides is crucial to consider or analyze before reaching a decision. No objective criteria strictly differentiate relevant information from irrelevant information. Policy decisions require subjective judgments concerning the best or most appropriate evidence. In our analysis, however, relevancy is limited by the appropriate applications of survey research methodology. Did participants learn the strengths and weaknesses of this tool or was it simply a convenient instrument for asking questions that could better (and more efficiently) be asked with some other research tool?

It is important to distinguish between *dissemination, utilization,* and *impact. Dissemination* refers simply to the act of sending information to a potential user; it occurs whenever information is transmitted. *Utilization* refers to the process by which information enters policy making. Information comes to the desk of a decision maker, it is read and understood, and it influences the discussion of policy. *Impact* is reserved for information that yields a documentable influence on a particular decision. In analyzing use, we relate the dissemination and use of information to a specific problem, policy area, or issue; for example, growth in housing, location of new federal housing projects, or the use of diet drugs. Thus, the policy questions, not the information request nor the act of utilization, represent the basic unit of analysis.

Summary

The model for analysis is not restricted to the analysis of the CNS experiment. It can be used in most applied research ventures involving interactions between sponsors, researchers, users, and the OMB; that is, in most applied research sponsored by the federal government.

The model requires one to employ a variety of data collection techniques including general detective work (tracing flows of information through the decision-making hierarchy) and asking general attitudinal and behavioral questions that enable one to specify an agency's overall information policy, the criteria of that policy, and its implementation.

Thus, application of the model of the knowledge-inquiry system and its operation produces several types of research results: a specification of constraints placed on the overall operation of the system, a description of the system's operation (actors participating, decisions made) for the time period analyzed, a description of the flows of information and patterns of utilization, an analysis of the factors affecting utilization, and an analysis of the actors' perceptions of the system's success.

CHAPTER 3

Development and Funding of the Survey Experiment

The Continuous National Survey (CNS) was part of a second generation of projects funded by the National Science Foundation (NSF) which provided support for applied research concerning the information needs of decision makers in government. The first generation of projects, in the late 1960s, were institutional support grants. NSF gave large grants (up to $4 million) to major private research institutions to underwrite present research and the development of new research. The intention was to support a permanent senior staff that could respond quickly to social crises. NSF hoped that some of this research would speak to the needs of federal policy-making agencies. Having a permanent staff, these institutions had the potential to be responsive to the immediate problems facing decision makers in Washington. As a problem emerged, these senior staffs could potentially respond with a research proposal.

Like many university-based research institutions (the Institute for Social Research, Stanford Research Institute), NORC applied for one of these grants; it was not, however, awarded an institutional support grant. The NSF program folded before NORC's proposal was considered. However, other institutions did receive support grants. In the winter of 1971, the new director of NORC went to Washington to meet with the director of NSF. He argued that it was unfair that NSF supported other institutions without making similar resources available to NORC. The director of the newly created RANN division was also at this meeting. The director of NSF asked the director of NORC and other staff members to meet with the RANN staff, with the understanding that some funding arrangement would be worked out.*

At the meeting with RANN representatives, NORC's director had two goals: to receive funding equal to that of other research institutions and to obtain a grant that would continue for two to three years, giving the center some flexibility in its staffing. At the initial meeting between RANN and NORC, RANN's representatives made it clear that its interests were very practical: "We operate under the slogan, Who is going to use it for what? Our grants are not for the purpose of giving professors funds." NORC was told that if it submitted a proposal for an applied social science research project within a relatively

---

*During the interviews, all respondents were promised confidentiality. Therefore, the identities and institutional affiliations of participants are not revealed. All quotations are taken directly from the tapes of recorded interviews. At all meetings during the initial stages of this project, individuals were speaking for their organizations. They either had the authority to make decisions for their agency or were to inform people of an agency position that could be modified only by a superior who was not present at the meeting in question. Thus, the statements made at these meetings by individual actors assumed an institutional character. Commitments were made in the name of the organization. At this stage of the project's development, individual statements that deviate from the organization's position cannot be determined. Because of the limited number of actors involved, they were viewed as identical. Thus, for example, when a RANN position is cited, it should be understood to include two components: the institutional character of the statement made and the limited number of individual actors involved at this stage of the development. On the basis of the interviews, it is clear that agency representatives perceived others as speaking for their agencies.

short period of time, RANN would give it "lots of money"; if not, "NORC would not get a nickel." RANN also said it was not interested in the traditional academic research proposals that take three to four years to complete: "Decision makers in Washington operate under radically different time constraints than social scientists do; they need to have answers quickly." However, at this meeting, RANN did not say that it would fund only a project directed at the needs of federal policy makers. RANN required that the potential users of the research results be specified in the proposal; these users could be at any level of government, as long as their interest in the proposed research was included in the proposal.

In the summer of 1971, the director of NORC submitted a first proposal to RANN. It called for three or four national surveys a year, for a period of five years, which would cover general social policy questions. NORC assumed that such questions were or should be of interest to federal policy makers. In September 1971, RANN rejected this proposal, citing four major problems with the approach. First, the substantive areas were too general and were not adequate to the specific policy needs of federal agencies: "They were the kinds of general social policy questions that any good sociologist should be concerned with." Second, the plan for analysis was more appropriate to the research interests of social scientists than to the practical needs of policy makers. Third, the fast turnaround time, which is critical to policy makers, was not a feature of the proposal. Fourth, RANN felt that although a national random sample was ideal for social science research, it might not yield enough information about specific target populations to speak to the needs of federal policy makers. As a representative of RANN put it: "National samples tend not to give enough breakdowns for policy makers. There is no agency in Washington that is concerned with Americans in general. Each is concerned with some small group like veterans, old people, students, and doctors."

The director of NORC then submitted several redrafts, which were also rejected by RANN. The staff of RANN felt that although NORC understood what was wanted, it was not being flexible enough in providing it. At this time, RANN gave serious consideration to terminating negotiations with NORC; however, because of NORC's reputation and because RANN had received few good proposals, RANN decided to send representatives to Chicago to attempt to negotiate a mutually acceptable proposal. One RANN representative said: "If we had enough good proposals, we wouldn't have gone to Chicago; because we didn't, we worked on the assumption that NORC had high promise even though they were high risk. . . . We were interested in NORC because we had no other place to put the money; there weren't enough proposals that were good and we turned money back in."

It is important to note NSF's skepticism with respect to NORC's proposal. Had RANN not been a new division, wishing to prove itself by working with nationally reputable organizations, NORC's proposal for a national survey might never have survived these initial rejections. That is, the Continuous National Survey was not funded because NSF or RANN was enthusiastic about the project and committed to making it work. Instead, RANN felt some pressure to use the money available, and since NORC submitted one of the more promising proposals at the time, it received careful attention. It was in the interest of RANN, as an organization, to initiate some projects and not have to report to Congress that money allocated for purposes of new research and development had not been spent. RANN's failure to fund research projects might have dampened Congress's enthusiasm for RANN, a new program.

For RANN, the Chicago meeting represented a crucial turning point in the funding process. At the meeting, a RANN representative suggested a new kind of sampling design, one that had never been used before by NORC, a *cluster sample*. The method was to focus specifically on neighborhoods as clusters. The subjective attitudinal data collected from the surveys were to be integrated with objective data on the same neighborhoods. The objective data would consist of factual information related to the various social services available in the neighborhoods, and were to be obtained from published and unpublished statistics, from sources such as the U.S. Bureau of the Census block statistics and the census of housing. Other data, like the condition of a housing unit, would be observed and recorded by interviewers in the field. By integrating the objective and subjective measures, new quality-of-life indicators could be constructed. For example, the objective data would include the number of bus stops in a neighborhood and the frequency of bus service. The subjective survey data would indicate how often people used the bus, how satisfied they were with the service, and any improvements they would like to see introduced. Similarly, the approach of integrating subjective and objective data could be applied to policy decisions relating to food stamps. One could compare attitudinal data with available employment statistics and statistics concerning distribution of the stamps.

The idea of a continuous, massive, multipurpose survey was also introduced at the Chicago meeting. The participants agreed that the overall theme for these surveys would be a "national evaluation of community services." The collection of attitudinal data at the level of clusters or neighborhoods for comparisons of objective conditions and attitudinal information was critical to RANN. The RANN staff felt that this kind of information would be useful to policy makers in validating known trends and trends hypothesized by the agencies. The idea of a consortium of federal agencies as users of the CNS was originated by NORC. NORC also stipulated that it would be able to ask a core set of questions on each of the surveys fielded. RANN was willing to fund a proposal that included these components.

After their visit to Chicago, RANN participants submitted a final report to RANN in which they outlined the strengths and weaknesses of the project. The following summarizes their report.

> Strengths: (1) Provides policy makers much needed information concerning citizens' attitudes towards public programs and performance. (2) Includes potential users in decisions about which information to collect—greatly enhances the probability of providing needed information and going about it in the right way. (3) Provides information

on a timely basis. (4) By working with the information needs of several agencies at the same time, NORC would realize economies of scale. (5) There are benefits from interactions with other federal agencies and the use of a common approach to solving issues. (6) Given the lack of experience with an opinion survey for the purposes of evaluating administrative programs, the project requires a "risk" period, a demonstration time.

Weaknesses: (1) There is no mechanism for officially allocating time among the many users. Some sort of advisory committee of participants should be set up for this purpose. If this mechanism were made explicit before the project began and if NSF devoted time to staffing and resources for this support mechanism, it could work. (2) If support of the survey is eventually to be transferred to agency users, users have to understand the experimental nature of the project. Users should be required to periodically evaluate the usefulness of the information and their uses of it. At a minimum, agency users should be provided with shadow prices against which they can evaluate the value of the information. They should know the cost of each piece of information received, even though they are receiving it for free. A shadow price system would help users in their later decision about whether to fund the survey themselves. (3) For many issues important to federal agencies the sample size is too small. Therefore data collectors must play a critical role in the analysis. Given the distribution of federal programs, NORC should consider weighting the sample toward low-income populations. (4) The proposed budget for this project is somewhat high.

Finding the Users

Before RANN would make a final decision on whether to fund this project, NORC was required to stipulate the interested users. A RANN representative was made responsible for nego-

tiating with the potential users and making the final arrangements with NORC. RANN was committed to finding four interested user agencies before awarding a grant to NORC. In making
the initial contacts with the potential user agencies, RANN relied on the Federal Council on Science and Technology Advisory Board. Most representatives to this board were members of
the research staff of the agencies, rather than policy makers.
The initial line agency response to the proposed CNS was "abys-
mal." RANN reported that the most difficult part of the funding process was interesting the agencies in the survey. RANN
representatives found themselves in a predicament—they were
both "assessors" for the purposes of funding and "advocates"
for purposes of interesting the agencies in the project.

In trying to sell the survey, NSF promised to monitor and
ensure the quality of the data provided. The participating
agency would specify the questions that suited their policy
needs, and NSF would pay for the NORC service for a period of
one year. Agencies wishing to continue the surveys after that
time would pay for it from their own budgets. During the meetings with the representatives of the various agencies, RANN representatives explained their perceptions of the unique goals of
the project: agencies would receive information quickly (quick
turnaround time), agencies would receive information about immediate and current problems, and the cluster design would enable agencies to integrate the survey information with their own
objective data.

RANN was able to interest only three agencies in the
CNS: Department of Transportation, Department of Agriculture, and the Office of Economic Opportunity. After some per-
suasion, the Department of Housing and Urban Development
became interested in the project. (Table 1 shows participating
agencies.) The biggest roadblock to attracting agencies was "getting the people to see beyond the immediate problem that was
of interest to them at the time." RANN could succeed only by
convincing agencies that the survey instrument was appropriate
to their problems. Most agency representatives, however, voiced
doubts about the usefulness of a survey based on a national
sample, raising questions similar to those RANN had asked

Table 1. Agencies Participating in the CNS Experiment

Phase 1 (Funding)	Phase 2 (Planning)	Phase 3 (Conduct of Research, Cycles 2-7)	Phase 4 (Conduct of Research, Cycles 8-13)
Office of Economic Opportunity	National Institute of Education	National Institute of Education	National Institute of Education
Department of Housing and Urban Development	Department of Housing and Urban Development	Department of Housing and Urban Development	Department of Housing and Urban Development
Department of Transportation	Department of Transportation	Department of Transportation	Department of Transportation
Department of Agriculture	Department of Agriculture (two agencies)	Department of Agriculture (one agency)	Federal Energy Office
	Office of Management and Budget	Office of Management and Budget	
	Food and Drug Administration	Food and Drug Administration	
		Federal Gambling Commission (brief period only)	

during the initial negotiations. RANN stated that "if it had not been for these three agencies, we would not have been able to go ahead with the funding." RANN was, however, encouraged by their interest. A typical response to the proposed CNS of these three potential users is: "The proposal strikes us as a promising means for the collection of more timely economic and social intelligence. We would like to explore the subject further and, if the details can be worked out to our mutual satisfaction, arrange to participate actively in it. Though I cannot provide a list of specific questions which we would like to see included in the survey, I can outline some of the areas of study we would like to see this information contributing to and, as you will note, at least some of the information needs will likely overlap the needs of other federal research operations."

The staffs of RANN and NORC had different perceptions of the success of these early meetings with potential participants. RANN felt that NORC did a "very poor job" in selling the research proposal: "NORC did not seem to work very hard." The RANN staff characterized the NORC representatives as aloof and unconcerned about agencies' participation. RANN also felt that NORC could have taken more initiative in arranging meetings with agencies. Representatives of NORC, however, felt that it was not their job to initiate meetings with agencies: "We were very surprised to find out how little the NSF knew about Washington. They seemed to have very few contacts." NORC was willing to attend any meetings that RANN arranged, but did not feel that it should take the initiative at that time. NORC also did not feel that it should tell the agencies what their interests should be; therefore, NORC did not take an aggressive or active posture at the meetings. The NORC staff involved in the planning of the CNS had the impression that the agency representatives they met did not fully understand the goals that the experiment was designed to achieve and, therefore, did not understand the survey's applications to their policy needs.

Despite these difficulties, RANN decided to fund the experiment because several federal agencies had shown interest in the project. An unusual triangular relationship between sponsor, producer, and users was beginning to form: RANN expected NORC to take more initiative; NORC expected RANN to be centrally involved in the coordination of the project; the agencies were unsure of whom to consult about problems of administration and coordination. RANN's and NORC's respective roles and functions were not well defined or commonly understood, a confusion that threatened the overall success of the project.

Before the final grant could be awarded, the Statistical Policy Office of the Office of Management and Budget (OMB) had to review the proposal for purposes of "clearance." It was the practice of the Statistical Policy Division that any government inquiry that requires more than nine individuals to furnish information must obtain OMB clearance. There was some question as to whether the CNS—as a grant—should be subject to OMB clearance. The Statistical Policy Office took the position that the CNS was definitely subject to clearance procedures and asked NSF to arrange for a meeting between representatives of NORC, RANN, OMB, and the agencies that would be using the survey. The Statistical Policy Office's position at this initial meeting, spring 1972, was that the proposal sounded interesting, but it "also sounded quite vague. It didn't seem like an easy job knowing the lack of sustained interest of policy makers in data." The staff also had some reservations about the proposed central theme for CNS, that is, the evaluation of human service delivery systems: "This could be too narrow." OMB worried that the surveys might duplicate other surveys already funded by these agencies. NSF then invited a representative of OMB to accompany other agencies on a site visit to Chicago: "They did not want to become involved at this stage, and as a result we just ran like hell with the final grant award." A RANN representative said: "We would keep them informed and just hope they wouldn't say anything." OMB was also offered a place on the questionnaire, and showed great interest in taking advantage of this opportunity.

In the summer of 1972, RANN decided to commit $983,900 to the Continuous National Survey for a period of eighteen months. The RANN representative who went to Chicago was more enthusiastic about this project than the other staff members were. He reasoned: "We had the users, we had the money, and we were confident that NORC would be as good as anybody in making the information useful to policy makers." The grant stipulated that NORC would be funded for six months of planning and twelve months of fieldwork. The surveys were to be fielded every three to four weeks. Each of these surveys would represent one cycle, and during the year in the field NORC was to complete thirteen cycles. The RANN staff agreed that the project should be considered "an experiment in the uses of social data for federal agencies, and should it be successful, further support would be picked up by the user agencies."

From RANN's perspective, the most important parts of the grant were:

> (1) NORC will draw a national probability sample designed to yield approximately 900,000 completed cases, the universe being that of the U.S. noninstitutional population eighteen years of age and over. The sample points will number 500 small geographical units. They can be thought of as "neighborhoods"—though we shall not require that a particular neighborhood have a socially accepted name or boundary. (2) The sample of 500 segments will be divided into five equivalent sections of 100 neighborhoods. Each of these sections will be divided into 25 units, each unit consisting of 360· persons from the 100 neighborhoods. (3) Beginning on January 1, 1973, one unit will be interviewed every week throughout the year, each particular neighborhood appearing in the sample five times a year (every eleventh week), with a sample of three to four cases per appearance and a total of eighteen cases per year. On January 1 of each subsequent year, a new cycle will begin. Whether or not neighborhoods will change from year to year is not yet decided. (4) Parts of the seventy-minute personal interview will be constant throughout; parts will change, say every three months; and a small part will be left open for ad hoc decisions. (5) "Objective" data on various systems' inputs will be obtained on the 500 neighborhoods through existing federal data, reports from the participating agencies and through field data collection. (6) Reports will be made to the client agencies through a variety of mutually agreeable means ranging from informal telephone calls noting an apparently interesting trend through a statistical series of "indicator" variables to detailed statistical analyses of particular topics.

Some members of the RANN staff were much more skeptical about the grant than the one who played the role of advocate for the CNS within RANN. These other members felt that integrating objective and subjective data was critical for the success of the project and NORC could not collect and analyze both subjective and objective data within the limits of its budget.

Despite these reservations and the very long funding process, the CNS was funded because of RANN's interest in testing the experimental aspects of the project. RANN was persuaded that the procurement and utilization of social science information using a multiagency, multipurpose questionnaire were more important than some reservations related to potential problems of implementation.

The final steps in implementing the grant were staffing the project at NORC, diversifying contacts with potential user agencies to involve nonresearch personnel and policy makers in the project, composing and pretesting the questions for the first cycle, beginning the collection of the objective data, receiving OMB clearance for the questions, and fielding the first cycle by January 1973. By summer 1972, a year and a half after NORC's initial proposal, NORC was ready to test whether the experiment could work.

Funding Process: Constraints on CNS

Before analyzing the success of the CNS (Chapter Four), we need to identify the constraints placed on the project by the nature of the funding process. Because of the skepticism in Washington about the CNS, RANN had to work very hard to interest representatives of the federal agencies in Washington. Only three agencies were initially interested, and RANN had to work very hard to convince a fourth. Because the service was free, individuals within the agencies interested in the CNS were able to commit their agencies to participating in the project without necessarily consulting their superiors in the decision-making hierarchy. Any resulting conflicts between the policy makers responsible for decisions concerning utilization and lower-level bureaucrats responsible for procuring the CNS information would definitely constrain the success of the project.

RANN and OMB also expressed some skepticism about

the project. Since RANN disputed the role of OMB from the beginning, OMB's reservations were not taken very seriously. NORC, however, rather than enjoying the cooperation of this powerful agency, would have to "prove itself" in order to gain OMB's support. OMB's reservations and its power in Washington could have undermined CNS before the field research began. RANN's reservations also served as a constraint on the success of the CNS. One member of the RANN staff was more enthusiastic than any others about CNS. However, that staff member left RANN, and CNS was to be administered by individuals who had strong reservations about the funding of the project. Certainly, these individuals' cooperation and understanding were not as great as those of the enthusiastic staff member. Moreover, the agencies were skeptical about the survey instrument itself. Their cooperation could also not be expected until NORC had proved itself. But, to some extent, such proof depended upon the cooperation of all participants.

RANN's skepticism concerning CNS exasperated the problem of defining the appropriate working relationships between the agencies, RANN, and NORC. The failure to clearly define roles created friction during and after the funding process. The agencies did not know to whom they should refer problems with CNS. Should they go directly to NORC or to RANN, the funding agency? Furthermore, the agencies were not sure about their legal relationship to NORC. It was not a contractor-client relationship, since the user agencies were not paying for NORC's services. But RANN did not see itself as the coordinator. Some agencies felt comfortable going directly to NORC; others prefered to funnel their communications through NSF and RANN.

RANN, however, was not comfortable with its role, especially after the staff member largely responsible for funding CNS left. RANN felt that NORC had to stand on its own merits and wanted the smallest possible role in the administration of the project. RANN consistently resisted initiatives on the part of agencies to put it in an administrative position. Despite this resistance, some agencies apparently felt more comfortable working with RANN, a fellow agency in Washington, than with

NORC itself. RANN's inability to make its position clear during the funding process served as a constraint.

However, RANN did not want NORC to view its relationship with the agencies as a contractor-client relationship. RANN expected NORC to serve as a consultant to the agencies. As a consultant, if NORC felt that agencies were making improper or inappropriate use of the survey, it was to disallow the agencies' request. Thus, RANN expected NORC to reword questions and not worry about funding considerations. NORC, however, did not feel fully comfortable with this position.

NORC, as well as some of the agencies, expected RANN to take a much more active role in the administration of the project: "After all, they knew their way around Washington, and we didn't." NORC wanted RANN to serve as coordinator, at least for the first six months of the project.

At the very least, one must conclude that there was a lack of clarity in defining the interagency relationships. Neither the agencies nor NORC were used to dealing with an indirect funding arrangement. At this stage of our analysis, we need not consider whether RANN's expectations with respect to NORC and the agencies were realistic. The tensions between these three groups served as a constraint on the success of the project.

The length of the period of funding was another potential constraint on the success of the project. NORC originally asked for three years and almost $3 million; it received eighteen months and less than $1 million. As a result, NORC felt that it was thrust immediately into the position of "selling itself" to the agencies and to OMB for future funding. NORC felt it could not afford to act as a consultant, as RANN expected. To ensure future funding, NORC felt it should assume a client-contractor relationship with the agencies.

In addition to the questions of definition of role, the funding process involved only the research personnel of participating agencies. RANN consulted the research personnel of the domestic agencies represented on a federal advisory board to locate the users. Because CNS was intended to respond to the needs of upper-level policy makers, RANN's reliance upon research personnel for implementation seems somewhat inappropriate. Maximum utilization of information by policy makers would seem to require that the policy makers participate in the initial decisions concerning the design of the project. CNS's ties with the research offices, rather than the policy offices, served as a potential constraint on the success of the experiment.

RANN, however, justified working with the research personnel by citing its institutional mission. RANN explained that it had been established as a division of NSF "in the first instance to compete with other research directors—not to cooperate with them. . . . [OMB] wanted us to be so successful as to drive the other millions devoted to research out into the open where they could be seen, by making them [other research directors] angry." RANN contended that these goals dictated putting NORC in contact with researchers in the decision-making hierarchy. However, RANN also explained that over time its attitude was changing. The staff now wanted to cooperate and coordinate their efforts with other agencies, rather than to compete with them. Thus, it would seem that RANN's justification did not represent the real reason that NORC was introduced into research offices and not to policy-making offices. RANN's method seems to have been determined by convenience, not by a specific institutional mission. RANN firmly believed that it had concentrated on agencies in which NORC could be successful in "fanning out" to the policy-making offices.

Of course, research offices within federal agencies are interested in promoting their own in-house information products. There is probably some truth to the competition-conflict model suggested by RANN. The research personnel could potentially control NORC's success in diversifying its contacts within these agencies. Presumably, the research offices could choose to isolate NORC from the policy makers.

Beyond the constraints already outlined, NORC had some internal problems that also influenced the project's success. NORC's initial concern, as outlined in the history of the funding process, seemed to be gaining funding comparable to that of its competitors. Since NORC had not received an institutional support grant, it was determined to receive a grant that would still supply some institutional support and funding for continuous longitudinal research in the research areas to be covered by the CNS. This concern was so strong that NORC was very flexible in its negotiations with RANN. It willingly accepted the cluster design and the method of integrating objective and subjective data, apparently without having first carefully analyzed the budget and staffing entailed. Thus, when CNS was funded, NORC did not have the staff to begin work immediately. Staff had to be hired and trained upon receipt of the grant in the summer of 1972. Such internal problems, if they delayed the implementation of the project, represent another potential constraint on the project. Timeliness is critical for federal decision makers; researchers who cannot meet deadlines are not trusted and not relied upon.

These constraints were not so great as to affect the validity of the quasi-experimental conditions specified in the design of the CNS project. However, as the project developed, NSF, RANN, and NORC would have to pay attention to some of the following conditions: the involvement of upper-level policy makers, NSF's role in the administration of the project, scheduling and punctuality in the development of the project, and the relationship between NORC and the participating agencies.

Summary

Let us consider what this phase of the CNS experiment reveals about one aspect of the knowledge-inquiry system: policy makers' procurement of information from sources external to the decision makers' agency. We can report some preliminary findings concerning the nature of the funding process and the relationship between researchers and funding organizations. Research institutions may submit proposals designed primarily to underwrite the longevity of their organization. The substantive research focus may, therefore, be of less importance than the level of funding sought. In this particular case, the CNS represented the largest project at NORC at the time.

The granting and potential user organizations, however, have their own expectations of a particular project, and these may differ from those of the research organization assigned to execute the project. If the discrepancy in expectations is sufficiently great, it may affect the ultimate use of the information. At the early stage of the CNS project's development, neither the agencies nor the research organization receiving the grant outlined specific expectations regarding the actual use of the information. The agency participants stated that survey information could potentially be of use to them, and the interest of potential users led RANN to fund the project. But the agencies were not required to articulate specific uses for the information, and NORC was not required to propose specific policy areas to which the information could be applied. These important decisions, related to the ultimate success of the project, were to be resolved during the course of the project's development.

Indeed, neither the funding organization nor the research organization was particularly enthusiastic about or committed to the substantive focus of the project. CNS received funding for reasons related as much to chance as to a design intended to maximize federal policy makers' use of social science information. Had more proposals been submitted to RANN at the time the CNS was being considered, it might never have been funded. Similarly, had NORC received an institutional support grant, it might not have been interested in CNS. As it turned out, the institutional interest of both groups was served by their establishing a working relationship. RANN needed to fund quality projects to justify its existence and large budget to Congress, and NORC needed large grants to maintain its competitive position.

However, the complexities of the funding process should not be overemphasized. On the basis of this case history and analysis, one should not conclude that the funding process reflects only the maximization of organizational self-interests. Organizational interests in protecting budgetary allocations seem to play a larger role in funding decisions than substantive policy positions. However, RANN was created with a particular institutional character; it was to fund research projects that were to be used by specifically designated users. There is no doubt that CNS was funded because it was consistent with these goals. Similarly, NORC, as a research organization, had a long history of serving federal agencies and had substantive interests in CNS.

The history of the funding and the establishment of working relationships between NORC and the other actors in the project does, however, raise the question of the relative importance of administrative survival and substantive policy in the formulation and implementation of information policy. Our subsequent analysis of the development of the CNS project will assess the importance of both factors.

CHAPTER 4

Planning
and Conducting
the Project

Our description of the development of the CNS project, based on the analytic framework presented in Chapter Two, concentrates on those aspects of the experiment that contribute to our general understanding of knowledge-inquiry systems. Our analysis of the CNS project focuses on those aspects of this particular experiment that pertain to applied research involving sponsors, OMB, applied research organizations (knowledge producers), and user agencies at the federal level.

Planning Stage

During the planning phase, several important events affected the overall nature and outcome of the experiment. First, the planning phase lasted four months longer than expected, due to problems in the agencies' articulation of their needs, the OMB clearance process, and NORC's difficulty in defining its relationship to NSF and the participating agencies. The lag time between initial meetings with potential user agencies, summer 1972, and the end of the planning stage, spring 1973, caused some agencies to lose interest in the experiment.

Moreover, as agencies met with NORC during this period, the proposed integrating theme of the project—the comparison of subjective and objective measures of neighborhood services— was dropped in favor of flexibility. Participating agencies were to explain what they wanted for each cycle. They could build indicators by repeating questions over time; they could devote all their time to one issue; they could ask a different set of questions each time. This development was approved by the OMB and by each of the participating agencies, but NSF did not agree with this decision.

NORC's Decisions About Approaching the Agencies. NORC's approach to relations with the participating agencies can be characterized by the objective of providing the most competent technical services available. This goal, however, implied that NORC would serve as a consultant—not as a simple outside contractor—in the formulation of questionnaires. In other words, NORC would not elicit information that it considered to be an inappropriate use of survey research methodology. Thus, NORC reserved the right to refuse agencies' requests for surveys that NORC deemed inappropriate. NORC would, in these cases, explain to the agency how it might best utilize this research tool to meet its needs. Obviously, NORC's approach would be impossible to implement in a contractor-client relationship.

Further, if agencies could not articulate their information needs, NORC would not try to do it for them. NORC felt it should not tell the agencies what their needs were, or even help them to define their needs, because NORC did not want the agencies to later argue that they were receiving information they had not requested. Clearly, NORC was trying to walk a very difficult line: on the one hand, to be more than a contractor but, on the other hand, not to assume responsibility for information procurement. NORC representatives summarized the approach in the following manner: "To be as professional and low-keyed as possible so as to lay out the facts and to always leave the fundamental role of preference expression and need determination in the clients' hands. We never told them they needed it or that they had to have it." We note that this approach does not resolve the problems concerning the roles of NORC and the agency participants.

Initial Meetings with Agency Participants. NORC held meetings with representatives of the federal agencies interested in the project in the summer of 1972. Some meetings were held in Chicago, at which agency representatives explored substantive areas of interest to their agency. At these meetings, NORC and agency representatives also discussed how CNS might be of use in offices other than the one of the representative attending the meeting. These meetings served to introduce the agencies to the NORC staff, and agencies expressed their reservations about the operations or design of the project and proposed a timetable for the receipt of NORC's services.

Subsequent to the Chicago meetings, NORC representatives went to Washington and made a presentation, to interested members of a particular agency, concerning the project's capabilities and NORC's plans for implementation. After these Washington meetings, NORC asked the agency representative to contact those who had shown interest in the project. Individual meetings were then arranged between NORC representatives and agency representatives to explore potential uses of the survey in the various offices of the agencies. NORC hoped it could diversify its contacts within these agencies by working with an insider.

The pattern of these initial meetings influenced NORC's success in diversifying within these federal agencies. One person within each federal agency served as a broker between agency participants and NORC. All communications with the agencies were funneled through this broker. In all but one case, this agency broker was the same person contacted by RANN during the funding process; in the other case, the broker was selected at the first Washington meeting. Thus, NORC was asking the agency to share responsibility and risk in guaranteeing diversified contacts and success.

The implications of this kind of arrangement had definite effects on the development of the project. NORC's future within an agency depended, to a great extent, upon the broker's interests in the project and position within the agency. Clearly, it was to NORC's advantage to have a coordinator within an agency; however, the broker arrangement could either diversify NORC's contacts or limit NORC's options and opportunities within these agencies. Brokers who were well respected and well placed within their agency could use their influence to support the interest of the CNS. But brokers who were not well placed or not well respected were likely to constrain NORC's opportunities within the agencies.

Furthermore, this kind of arrangement also raises questions about the allegiances and objectivity of the brokers. If a broker is more interested in the project and its survival than are other agency personnel, the broker may be perceived by other personnel as unable to objectively assess the role of the project within the agency. If NORC were strongly tied to this broker, it would suffer from the agency's unwillingness to trust the objectivity of the broker's judgment. Further, in order for NORC to succeed in diversifying within an agency, it needed a realistic picture of communication patterns and expectations of agency participants. Brokers with vast research experience would be able to communicate easily with NORC, but if the brokers' research experience were atypical of other agency personnel, NORC would not gain a representative sense of the agency.

NORC had hoped that these initial meetings with agency participants would be completed by the beginning of October 1972. A draft of the first questionnaire would then be written, submitted to OMB for clearance, and pretested so that the first survey could be in the field, as scheduled, in January 1973. However, these initial meetings were not completed by October 1972, because of the difficulty NORC experienced in establishing relations with one of the agencies initially interested in the project and the great difficulty most of the agencies had in defining and articulating their research needs.

Agency Participation: Patterns and Motivations. NORC relied upon the agency brokers to establish contact within the participating agency. Thus, with one exception, NORC's initial contacts were limited to the research agencies of particular departments. These research agencies were typically under the supervision of the departments' assistant secretary for evaluation, research, and development. In the other case, NORC established contact with the office of a special assistant to the department's secretary.

Standard procurement procedures mandate that an assistant secretary approve any requests for new information resources, since he or she is responsible for allocating funds for research and development. Researchers must demonstrate the direct significance of the requested information to the problem-solving agenda of the agency in order to receive the assistant secretary's approval. This pattern of careful scrutiny and consideration was not followed in the case of the CNS.

Agency participants realized that, as with other procurements, the main purpose of CNS was to provide policy-relevant information. Participants who were trying to interest others in the project wrote memos that described the policy relevance of CNS in the following manner: *"Policy Relevance.* With the exception of a standard set of demographic and household questions, the survey questions originate with the participating agencies. Program agencies are to have ready access to ask policy questions for which timely survey results could be useful." One agency attempted to be more specific about this point, writing: "As evidenced by the questions on the NORC draft survey, we recommend that the initial survey treat only the two highest-priority topics on our list and that we turn to the other issues later in the survey year, as the opportunity arises. Though tentative questions have been submitted to NORC on all the topics listed, they will obviously have to be refined, checked for duplication, and reviewed by your office before becoming a part of the survey." Thus the agencies did not clearly delimit policy relevance; policy-relevant information, as perceived by these policy makers, was information related to their "high-priority, problem-solving needs."

Because the CNS service was free, either the assistant secretaries gave minimal attention to it and were willing to experiment or researchers interested in it contacted NORC without the prior approval and scrutiny of the assistant secretary's office.

Clearly, the motivations of agency personnel interested in CNS were somewhat different than those for projects that must go through the normal procurement procedures. The four brokers expressed the following motives for their participation:

I am convinced of the merits of this kind of project.

Our program agencies do not base many of their decisions on good information. Most of these agencies do not have a research organization of their own to serve their needs. I saw this as a mechanism for showing them that they could get answers to questions they were interested in on a whole range of issues.

I personally have a long background with survey research and thought that this would be useful to the agency.

It was a free good and therefore there were no costs involved in introducing this to the agency.

I have a strong interest in having survey research play a strong role in policy formulation.

I was interested in the project because we had all kinds of things we needed data on.

Since we were strapped for money, this project had the virtue of allowing you to experiment with question formulation when you were not sure how to ask something.

It was a damn sight more convenient than anything else available.

I especially liked the fact that it was free and that it could be plugged into any time a problem came up.

By virtue of my own training I knew what

the utility of this kind of tool would be for my agency.

The quick turnaround time promised by NORC is a big asset.

All four brokers exhibited a strong positive relationship between their background with survey research and their motivation to participate. Some of their motives are consistent with and supportive of the experimental nature of CNS. RANN wanted agencies to experiment with different kinds of information, with data that were not obtained through the standard procurement process. CNS was designed to generate support for the idea of a multiagency project that would allow agencies to ask questions as they occurred on a short-term basis. Thus, some deviation from the normal procedures was built into the design of the project. In addition, it was natural that agency participants experienced in survey research would be the ones to facilitate their agency's participation. However, CNS was not designed to bypass standard approval procedures. But the assistant secretaries and other upper-level policy makers were brought into the project only after an initial decision had been made to participate. Moreover, the brokers' patterns of motivation do not reflect the careful thought and time usually given to new information requests. Thus, while the experimental components are consistent with the design of the CNS project, the deviations from standard information-gathering procedures are not.

The major difference in motivation between the brokers and other agency participants who became involved during the planning stage was the focus upon policy-relevant information. This desire was, with one exception, only implicit in some of the brokers' comments: "I knew what the utility would be to the agency," and "Our program agencies did not have good information." The other interested participants were much more explicit about this concern: "I wanted to use the survey to get at fundamental policy questions," and "When a policy decision comes up, we rely upon the judgments of people. The survey should enable us to assess whether these people are using sound judgment." Again, these differences reflect the fact that the usual criteria for policy relevance were not carefully applied when initial interest was shown in the CNS. Even those who expressed concern over policy relevance did not explicitly define the term. These differences reflect RANN's initial concern: that researchers and policy makers have different agendas and different approaches to problem solving.

Agency Participation: NORC's Contacts. NORC had developed a strategy for diversifying within the participating agencies—it worked with a broker responsible for contacting colleagues and coordinating their participation. If NORC was to have a long-term relationship with an agency, it had to succeed in moving beyond its initial contacts.

Two of the agencies introduced CNS into their program offices and into the office of the secretary. In one case this diversification was due to the strategic place of the broker; in the other, it represented a response to the initial Washington meeting. In the other two agencies, the project did not establish working relationships beyond the office in which it was introduced. (See Appendix B for a summary of the development of working relationships.) In the cases in which the project was successful in diversifying, staff members of other program agencies were frequently involved in the project; this participation included regular meetings with NORC, some meetings with the broker within the agency, and some telephone conversations with NORC. During this stage of development, most communications with NORC were funneled through the agency broker. Some general policy offices were involved, and their staff members also frequently participated in the project. However, the upper-level policy makers (the assistant secretary and secretary) did not have any direct contact with the project. In one agency, upper-level policy makers were told only that the project existed; in the other, there was no direct or indirect involvement. However, in one agency, a special assistant to the secretary showed the same kind of involvement and attention as the program agencies. These high-level staff people were involved in formulating the survey questions during meetings with NORC in Washington and in telephone conversations.

Agency Participation: Questionnaire Formulation. The

discussions concerning the questions to be used for the pretest and the first cycle took place after the initial Chicago and Washington meetings. In these discussions, the brokers served as coordinators in that they knew how many minutes were allocated to an agency and could decide how to distribute the time among the various interested agencies. This role was quite important in the two agencies in which the project had succeeded in diversifying. In the other two, the brokers simply took responsibility for determining which substantive policy areas would be covered by the first set of questions.

The formulation of the questionnaire was completed in one of two ways. Agency participants communicated to NORC general policy or programmatic problems that were facing the agency, and NORC drafted a set of questions to be reviewed by these participants; or the agency participant drafted a set of questions and asked NORC to rework them. During a subsequent meeting between NORC and the agency, they hammered out the final questionnaire. In some cases, the agency participant specified the policy problem of interest but still expected NORC to draft the questionnaire. The major differences between these processes are the specificity of the agencies' substantive requests and the amount of written material submitted by them. In all cases, NORC was responsible for formulating the final questionnaire.

For the pretest and first cycle, seven participating agencies were interested in asking questions about seven different policy areas: HUD, DOT, OMB, NIE, two agencies within DOA, and FDA.

Some tensions began to develop between NORC and the agencies during the completion of the formulation process. First, NORC was very unhappy about the lack of clarity and specificity on the part of some agency participants. As already noted, NORC took the position that it would not articulate or specify problems for the agencies. Thus, the formulation of the questionnaire, scheduled to take one month, took three months. One agency did not communicate any requests until November 1972. Second, a number of agencies could not effectively manage the long-distance relationships involved in formulating the questionnaire. Several participants felt that NORC should have established a Washington office to allow day-to-day communication. Third, some agency participants felt that NORC had not properly staffed the project. They wanted a policy analyst on the NORC staff to help the agencies articulate their needs and translate them into research language. Fourth, some agency participants felt that they should be able to ask questions about any subject they felt to be appropriate. NORC, however, insisted that it decide what was appropriate. Fifth, agency participants felt that if NORC better understood the problems to be addressed, then there would be no dispute about what was appropriate. Sixth, and related to this, some agency participants felt that NORC was learning as much or more about the federal government than the agencies were about survey research. To the extent this was true, NORC could not be a valuable resource to the agencies. In other words, NORC did not possess knowledge of the rules and procedures that governed bureaucratic life in Washington, and thus it could not fulfill the function of a government resource.

Regarding the substance of the questions, three options were discussed. First, questions about ongoing, long-term concerns of the agency; these questions would be asked over a number of cycles and would be monitored for variations over time. Second, experimental questions that might improve the question formulation process and lead to the development of new indicators over a period of time. A test set of questions would be compared with data produced by other agency methods. The test questions would be refined until a valid indicator was produced. Third, questions around "hot" issues, those problems of immediate concern to the agencies.

Agency participants differentiated most clearly between general policy and programmatic concerns. The programmatic concerns involved evaluations of specific public services provided by the department in question. The agency participants proposing these questions were required to do so, by law, and generally were not sure how the information would be used by their supervisors. In general, however, they indicated that the programmatic concerns were not high-priority items in terms of the day-to-day problem-solving needs of their superiors. For example, questions of how to best deliver food stamps to clients are important to lower-level program administrators, but would not come to the attention of higher-level policy makers unless they had to formulate or rewrite enabling legislation or testify before Congress. Some general policy concerns did speak to the immediate needs of policy makers: general broad guidelines on inflation, energy conservation, food production, or transportation systems.

The initial questions proposed by agency participants are easily categorized. The majority were evaluative in nature; for example, Do you feel that our television program is a success? Would you prefer this option to another? The next most frequent category was social inventory or factual questions: How many cars do you own? How often do you travel to this city? Do you take drug X? Least frequently asked were attitudinal questions: Who is at fault for the energy crisis? Generally, the social inventory and factual questions were used for monitoring purposes, or less frequently for developing indicators, the evaluative questions for the "hot" issues, and the attitudinal questions for a little bit of each.

All the proposed questions represented ongoing concerns of the agencies. They were not simply research questions of interest to a few individuals, nor were they purely academic in nature. With one exception, each participant had clear expectations as to how the information fit the overall information-gathering activities of the agency and how the information would be used. (See Appendix C for sample questions proposed by federal agencies.)

Each kind of question was thought of as fulfilling a different need and, therefore, had different implications in terms of ultimate utilization. The social inventory and factual questions would be used for ongoing policy formulation and review of programs as well as for helping to build a data bank that would be useful for periodic evaluations. The attitudinal questions were thought of as providing general background for the agencies, helping personnel understand how the public was thinking. They would, therefore, be used for general briefing of those responsible for decision making. The evaluative questions were of central concern to program administrators, whose expectations concerning use were the most vague and ill defined of all the participants. They felt only that in some general sense "the information was going to help assess program development and possibly contribute to the process of regulation writing."

A typical program administrator described the usefulness of his proposed questions in a memo, here excerpted:

> The food program topic was ranked first for several reasons. First, though the program has grown rapidly over the past few years (over $3 billion budgeted for 1973), very little reliable information is available concerning the size of the program's target population, its performance in reaching that population, characteristics of participants, reasons for nonparticipation, overlap with other forms of welfare assistance, and the like. Furthermore, there is ample evidence that the survey information is wanted and would be used. The administrator of the agency has himself participated in the design of questions. Thus, the surveys offer an opportunity to demonstrate that relevant information can be collected and be made available for decision making in a relatively short span of time.
>
> The questions on housing were given high priority for somewhat the same reasons, though in this case the questions originated within the secretary's office rather than within the administering agency. Again, this is a program that has grown rapidly over the past four or five years with loans in 1973 exceeding $2 billion . . . more so than most people appreciate. For example, though only 32 percent of the occupied building units in the United States were located in areas served by this program in 1970, 68 percent of all units in the nation that lacked complete plumbing were located there. And when "substandard housing" is defined as incomplete plumbing or overcrowded units, rural areas account for just under half of the U.S.

total. The questions included in the survey are designed to help determine: the opportunity for shifting program funds away from new housing starts and toward repair and renovation; attitudes toward mobile homes; the demand for rental housing in rural areas; citizen awareness of the Farmers' Home Administration housing loan program; and the relationship between residential mobility and the availability of housing. These are policy questions upon which decisions will be made within the coming months.

Those agency participants concerned with more general policy concerns were more specific:

We propose to use two cycles of the RANN survey for questions about community control of public schools. Ever since the controversy over Ocean Hill-Brownsville, the community control issue has entered into policy discussions at all levels of government. But our search of ERIC and other sources of educational research literature reveals little good evidence about how much "community control" people want, and what are the characteristics of the people who support it, and how strongly the concern is felt in the general population. We have designed a set of survey items to gather evidence from NORC's national sample on the following questions:

- Do those who favor community control favor full operating control over the schools, full control over special aspects of school policy, or simply more influence than they have now (but not complete control of anything)?
- How widespread is the opinion that citizens have too little influence in school policy? Are there some groups in which that opinion is especially relevant?
- Among those who are in favor of more citizen influence, what aspects of school policy are considered the most important to control or influence?

- Does past or present level of participation in civic affairs affect a respondent's likelihood of favoring more citizen control of schools? What about the relationship between satisfaction with the way schools are now being run and the respondent's sentiments about community control?

The use of the data produced from these questions was taken into consideration by most of the participants. However, they were not able to define the expected uses beyond the most general concerns. Some agencies also tried to put their information needs in the context of the overall goals of the program. A typical memo of this kind listed the specific information needs in a condensed form followed by an interpretation of the experimental goals of the project:

1. Food programs
2. Rural housing
3. Food prices
4. Residential preference (to be introduced later in the survey year)
5. Information and communication
6. Retail food distribution
7. Public attitudes toward agriculture
8. Environmental attitudes (being developed now)

Probable NSF and NORC Selection Criteria
1. Overlap of interest with other participant agencies
2. Merits of the issue—number of persons affected, how affected, appropriateness of federal intervention, and the like
3. Opportunity for survey results to have direct impact on program administration and policy making
4. Experimental attitude with the opportunity for results to influence future use of the survey technique
5. Capitalizes on survey uniqueness regarding the opportunity to collect "trending" information and to alter questions through time

Finally, we note that NORC made the final decisions concerning the format of the questions for each cycle. The first portion of each cycle was to be devoted to NORC's questions, which were concerned with basic demographic information and attitudes and perceptions concerning aspects of neighborhood and community life. The second portion consisted of the agencies' questions, finalized with the NORC staff, on the concerns of its policy makers.

OMB Clearance Procedures. A draft of the questionnaire was completed at the end of November and was submitted to the Statistical Policy Division of OMB for clearance. Agency relations with OMB are generally strained. Agency participants tended to characterize OMB as "picky," "a nuisance," "not understanding the programmatic needs of the agencies," "biased," "power hungry," and as "people who simply enjoy holding meetings." Other agency participants felt that OMB was interested only in gaining a bigger place for itself on the questionnaire. Obviously, there was a great deal of resentment toward OMB.

Clearly, the agency participants were not anxious to take a leading role in negotiations with OMB; nor were they willing to risk their status or position with OMB in a battle over a new information resource that was yet unproven. Neither was NSF willing to play a major role in this process. The primary responsibility fell to NORC.

OMB rejected the first draft of the questionnaire submitted. The OMB staff felt that agencies were asking questions that they already had enough information about from other studies, that there was no direct policy relevance to many of the questions, and that questions were vague and not clearly worked out. OMB also argued that it did not see the value of collecting much of the information proposed in the first draft of the questionnaire. However, OMB seemed most concerned about NORC's section of the questionnaire.

NORC was very frustrated by this first encounter with OMB. The CNS staff was put into the position of justifying the proposed questions and changing them to gain clearance. NORC also became very concerned that OMB's objections would result in further delays in completing the planning stage. NORC arranged a meeting with all of the participating agencies, OMB, and those consultants OMB had contacted with respect to the questionnaire. At that meeting, OMB stated that the quality of the questionnaire did not indicate that the agency participants were "taking seriously their use of this information resource." Agencies argued that some of the information was needed immediately for policy formulation and legislation; their urgency helped ensure the viability and success of the project.

After the meeting, NORC helped each agency draw up a memorandum outlining their information needs and their importance. NORC tried to respond to OMB's concerns by adding some policy questions to its section and by making it shorter. This process of writing agency memos and consulting with OMB continued until clearance was finally granted in May 1973.

Both NORC and the agencies were very frustrated by the length of time it took to gain clearance. Both felt that OMB was acting in a destructive manner rather than giving constructive advice. The long clearance procedure reflected the tensions between the agencies and OMB concerning who should control the procurement of information and what information should be gathered. The agencies felt that they, and not OMB, should control the information gathering.

Some of these tensions were manifested in the discussions over duplication and overlap in procuring CNS information; OMB was not willing to allow any duplication. One program administrator wrote a memo to the OMB staff expressing these concerns:

> At the time of my first exposure to this project, my perception of its potential role was much as you described it in our meeting last month. To wit, it seemed to offer an opportunity to experiment with survey techniques for the collection of policy-relevant information. But the more I talk with program administrators and policy makers, whom I visualize as the principal consumers of this product, the more I feel that the real value of this

project lies in its demonstration of existing survey tools rather than experimentation with new ones. To the statistician or the researcher this doesn't offer much excitement; in fact, it is downright pedestrian. But to the program administrator who lacks an analytical staff arm and who has had little if any experience in applying public opinion information to his decision process, the prospect is promising if not exciting. The information needs reflected in the department's submissions come not from the analysts and researchers but from those who will use the information. If they ask for information that already exists, this itself says something about the responsiveness of our current systems for collection and dissemination.

Thus, the tensions between OMB and the agencies were more fundamental than simple conflicts over duplication of information. They reflect different attitudes toward information procurement in general. The agencies wanted to participate in a process focused on their needs and supervised under their control, but the OMB staff was interested in encouraging multi-agency coordination and control in information procurement. NORC was convinced that "the reason they denied clearance was to get the attention of the agencies which were participating and convince them that, by participating in this project, they were not avoiding the OMB clearance process."

NORC also discovered, during the planning stage, that there was "an art to gaining OMB clearance": "One had to behave in such a way so as to acknowledge the significance of their comments; this is the equivalent of changing your item wording or adding items at their behest, or deleting items at their behest, no matter what the significance of those items are in a conceptual sense." NORC became aware of the flexibility that was necessary in dealing with OMB and the necessity of acknowledging their coordinating role, rather than fighting about it. This recognition led to the development of very good working relationships between the CNS staff and the Statistical Policy Division. After the first clearance process was completed,

OMB stated that subsequent clearance could be handled informally over the phone, without interference. Obviously, the agencies were very pleased that NORC had become so adept in dealing with OMB. But they remained generally frustrated by the central control and coordination functions exercised by OMB.

The Role of NSF and RANN. The delays in the clearance process and the planning stage are at least to some extent related to the roles adopted by NSF and RANN. RANN was not willing to intervene with OMB and refused to coordinate the CNS project. Despite attempts by NORC and the agencies to involve RANN in the arbitration and resolution of some of the tensions arising during the planning stage, RANN was unwilling to change its position: "It was essential that the agencies and NORC work out a direct working relationship which was independent of any RANN involvement."

Given the nature of NSF as the funding agency, both NORC and the participating agencies felt RANN should aid them in establishing these working relationships. They felt that RANN, as a federal agency concerned with applied research, understood the problems related to policy makers and that, as a research group, RANN could communicate with NORC. Furthermore, they felt that tensions of the kind experienced were detrimental to the development of the project and could have been resolved more quickly had RANN intervened. Some agency participants characterized RANN's position as "irresponsible." NORC felt that "on a practical level, this lack of willingness or ability to take on a dynamic leadership role with respect to the other participating agencies was a significant negative factor in the development of the project." But RANN's own skepticism about CNS and its early conflicts with NORC only made it firmer in adhering to its position.

NORC's Definition of Its Role. During this phase, the director of NORC decided that he could not work full-time on CNS. Thus, a new study director was hired to administer the project—including developing and maintaining relationships with participating agencies.

NORC's biggest problems, during this phase of the project, were with NSF. The redefinition of the óbjective data component by the new study director caused an irreparable rift with NSF. RANN felt that the objective component was the most attractive part of the grant, but doubted NORC's ability to fulfill that portion of the grant. However, NORC did not understand why RANN was so insistent about this component of the project: "They were basically annoyed with us because they wanted to have this so-called independent variable data which, for some bizarre reason, they seemed to have decided is the world's path to salvation."

In outlining its position more fully, NORC argued that if RANN insisted on having this objective information collected, it would cost them another half million dollars and that "these so-called objective measures are not and never will be correlated with subjective measures, and the reason isn't that we are doing a bad job of measurement." The new study director described the notion of integration as "extraordinarily simple-minded" and added, "It is inconceivable to me that human beings would reflect in any regular functional way certain characteristics of their environment." NORC felt that although the notion of integrated data had a great deal of currency in Washington policy-making circles, CNS should not be burdened by trying to implement notions "that are that stupid."

NORC's arguments with respect to this substantive matter were not accepted by NSF or RANN. RANN noted that NORC agreed to deliver this particular substantive product when it accepted the grant. Therefore, NORC had to meet the terms of the grant at no additional cost to NSF. That the newly hired NORC study director did not value the substantive component was an internal matter for NORC to resolve, and his objections did not affect the basic terms of the grant. When the participating agencies and OMB agreed with NORC, RANN dropped the matter. Nevertheless, this issue created tensions that affected NSF's approach to the project; it created a feeling among the RANN staff that NORC was not acting in good faith.

Discussion: The Importance of the Planning Stage. The planning stage of the CNS is particularly significant because it reflects the constraints put on CNS by the funding process. The actions of the primary participants during the planning phase are consistent with the patterns established during the funding period. More importantly, new patterns established during the planning stage influenced NORC's success in diversifying its contacts within agencies, the criteria by which agencies would evaluate NORC's services, and the agencies' ultimate decision about funding CNS once the grant money was no longer available.

Despite these difficulties, the completed questionnaire did speak to a variety of policy concerns and both long-term and short-term needs. The formulation of the questionnaire did follow the experimental guidelines to the extent that specific utilization plans were considered. Research staff members had selected policy areas to which the information would be applied, but program staff members were less clear about utilization.

The difference between research and program staff presents two distinct problems that needed to be resolved in future stages of development: Would the appropriate policy makers be convinced of the research staff's assumptions? If the program personnel could not define uses for CNS information, would the project have a future in those agencies? The latter is an especially important concern for program agencies because they do not have ongoing data analysis components. Therefore, if program staff could not point directly to a use for CNS data, CNS would not have a future within that agency.

The planning stages also demonstrated that NORC needed to learn governmental rules and procedures, for example, the clearance process and the expectations of federal participants. Although CNS staff did not initially understand (and even resented) the OMB clearance procedures, they later established a good, solid working relationship that continued for the duration of the project. CNS staff also learned the necessity of diversifying within any agency.

The planning phase of the project also illustrates the importance of analyzing the knowledge-inquiry system from the perspective of each of the major actors. When the agendas of these actors conflict, delays and difficulties are inevitable. Because of the delays, NORC seemed likely to face cost overruns.

The Conduct of Research

After the planning stage was completed, CNS was prepared to go into the field and begin to collect information. In the spring of 1973, the first cycle was fielded, and subsequent cycles were completed monthly. NORC's grant funds were depleted by December 1973, after six cycles; the original grant, however, was expected to fund thirteen cycles. The most significant events during this phase of the project were NORC's attempts to continue to diversify within the participating agencies, NORC's realization that the funds allocated for one year of fieldwork would be depleted after six or seven cycles, and the agencies' initial evaluations of NORC's work.

Agency Participation: NORC's Continued Diversification. During this stage of development, NORC diversified its contacts to include thirteen new staff participants and nine upper-level policy makers, including participants from one new department (Federal Energy Office) and a government research institute, FDA, which was not involved during the planning stage. These new participants were applying their energies to fourteen new policy areas. (See Appendix B for a summary of these developments.)

NORC also tried, unsuccessfully, to diversify into the secretary's offices in two other departments. Obviously, the initial constraint of being dependent upon research offices for establishing contact with a department was not hindering the CNS's ability to diversify within the agencies. Indeed, policy makers' contact with the project was more intensive during this stage of development. In two of the agencies, the secretary and assistant secretary received reports summarizing the results of the project. In one case, the assistant secretary and secretary received a briefing concerning the project from the staff coordinator. The upper-level policy makers did not take sufficient interest in the project, at this stage, to become involved in questionnaire formulation or other operational concerns. The policy makers' input was limited. Although secretaries are not usually involved in administrative matters concerning the day-to-day operations of projects, if they were sufficiently interested, it would not be unusual for them to give direction to questionnaire formulation. Assistant secretaries usually offer more direct substantive input and, although their offices would not want to be involved in day-to-day operations, decisions concerning questionnaire formulation and kinds of reports could be dealt with frequently if sufficient interest were shown.

At the staff level, the brokers continued to play a major role. They were the only ones who regularly met with NORC; others continued to funnel communications through them. In the organizations newly involved with CNS, the broker role was less pronounced, because CNS failed to interest a person within these agencies in adopting the role.

The staff members who were not brokers met with NORC representatives when they were in Washington, occasionally met among themselves concerning the project, and telephoned NORC more frequently than they had during the planning stage. However, their contact was still significantly less intense than the brokers'.

Some of the brokers became uncomfortable with their position during this period. They felt that NORC was relying upon them too heavily and that they "could not devote their careers to this project." One commented that he felt like a "trained seal": every time the project came up in a discussion or a meeting, he said positive things. He began to feel that, in the future, his opinion concerning the procurement of information might be discounted on this basis. NORC encouraged these brokers to take a lead role. The CNS staff felt it was improper for them to assume this role themselves.

Agency Participation: Questionnaire Formulation. In substance none of the new proposed questions reflected methodological planning concerns or the development of indicators. Nine of the fourteen new policy areas concerned program evaluation, and the other five were general policy issues of immediate concern to the agencies. The policy areas introduced in the planning stage were represented by the same kinds of questions as before. Six of the seven sets of questions were repeated for another cycle and one set was dropped. The two most significant substantive developments in the questionnaire formulation were the use of the survey to assess public behavior concerning the energy crisis and the coordination among three of the participants in formulating questions concerning energy. At least in this one area, the agencies were able to use the instrument as intended.

Moreover, in the new policy areas, the utilization concerns were more clearly defined and intense than they had been during the planning stage. Even though upper-level policy makers did not directly contribute to question formulation, the agency staff were reflecting the concerns of these policy makers, as expressed during agency staff meetings. The staff proposing the questions no longer had to guess which topics would or should be of interest to policy makers. They now relied less on their intuition and more on upper-level policy makers' statements. Yet, the program staff were still not able to define the use to be made of the information collected as often as the other participants.

Tensions Between NORC and the Agency Participants. CNS's success in diversifying, both in terms of new contacts and new policy applications, did not resolve the tensions between it and the participating agencies. In some cases, tensions intensified and new ones developed. The new tensions centered around the form of NORC's written reports to the agencies, the length of time it took NORC to submit these reports, and NORC's having run out of funds before completing all the fieldwork.

NORC took the position that the written reports should include only simple cross tabulations, some explanation of the methodology, and a verbal summary of the cross tabulations. NORC said it did not have the resources to produce more sophisticated analyses or to shorten the turnaround time and that it was not appropriate for it to interpret the results in terms of policy. Only the agencies, with their background and expertise in these policy areas, could provide the appropriate interpretations. The agencies found that NORC's position raised very serious problems. First, all participants believed that if

NORC had a regular contract with the agencies, more sophisticated analysis and interpretation would have been required. Moreover, NORC would have been required to give oral briefings to a large group of policy personnel. Since NORC's services were not paid from agency funds, the agencies did not feel they could place such requirements on NORC. However, they would eventually judge and compare NORC with other information resources.

Second, when NORC did not achieve fast turnaround time (that is, reports within three weeks after the fieldwork was completed) for the vast majority of participants, the agencies expected that the delayed reports would contain more analysis. When they did not receive a fuller analysis, they felt that NORC was performing below par. In the energy-related policy areas, NORC did begin to produce weekly reports during this stage of the project. In addition, at times daily conversations took place between agency participants and the CNS staff. Agency participants observed that it was possible for NORC to meet short-term demands. Several agency participants claimed that NORC was favoring one group of clients over another, that NORC was giving the greatest attention to those participants most likely to continue to fund the survey.

Moreover, some agency participants felt that the CNS staff should not devote additional time to agencies that had not best learned how to use the instrument. Instead, the CNS staff should ensure that all participants were able to make the best use of the survey. Staff members from the CNS told us: "The sense that people probably perceive favorites is along the lines of who do we give our time to and at what point; we always decided that based on perceptions of need. . . . Our perception of the situation was that putting time in with certain agencies was probably close to the equivalent of staying in bed because of their internal condition: namely, there was no pay-off. There were no new things happening at those agencies because they weren't putting in the time on the project."

Furthermore, NORC took the position that it would continue to decide the appropriate uses of the survey instrument. If the CNS staff thought that an agency was not making proper use of the instrument and did not have the potential to do so, then they spent less time with that agency. NORC did not view itself as playing favorites, but rather using effectively the time available. The CNS staff believed that those agencies that did not know what they wanted and did not devote time to the project perceived the project as "very flippant" during the grant period, and would perceive allocating money to the project as producing more flippancy.

The most serious tension occurred over the issue of the cost overrun. Even the brokers who became close allies of the CNS during this period were quite upset by NORC's failure to meet its budget constraints. All agency participants felt that NORC did not understand the implications of this budgetary matter and "did not take it seriously enough." The planning period made higher-level agency participants skeptical about NORC's ability to meet the budget. NORC's failure to warn the agencies of the overrun and its magnitude made the tensions even greater. NORC would complete only about 60 percent of the fieldwork promised: "Yet, they wanted to operate as if this were simply an oversight on their part," an agency official complained.

The tensions related to the overrun were intensified when the agencies were asked to make a budgetary evaluation before they had adequate results on which to judge CNS. NORC's handling of the overrun and its failure to adhere to the schedules were "inconceivable" to most agency participants. However, NORC felt that the agencies had contributed as much to these problems as it had. After all, the agencies had difficulty in defining their needs and were no more successful than NORC in negotiations with OMB. NORC's solution was to propose such a high budget that an overrun "simply could not occur." The agency participants seemed to conclude that NORC was technically very competent but could not administer a project.

Summary

Overall, our description of this stage of development reaffirms the importance of adhering to established agency organizational rules and procedures. The most important events were the tensions arising from the role of the brokers and NORC's inability to comprehend the importance of organizational rules. Cost overruns and delays in meeting schedules are not important events in and of themselves. The government is certainly not free of them. However, organizational procedures demand that contractors and grantees adhere to the initial terms mutually agreed upon "to the best of their ability." This stipulation implies that meeting schedules is important and a cost overrun of the magnitude of the CNS experiment is unacceptable. Even the stronger supporters of the CNS thought that the cost overrun was critical, but NORC was embedded strongly enough in their agencies that the staff did not withdraw their support.

Regarding this phase in the development of the CNS as a knowledge-inquiry system, several points are clear. The CNS was not meeting all the experimental conditions specified in the literature, defined in the experiment, and described in the RANN guidelines. Although CNS was providing information recognized as relevant by all parties, it was not in all cases delivering reports on schedule; the cost estimates specified in the grants were not adhered to; and participants disagreed on the form of the reports. Were these conditions, as the literature on the two cultures would suggest, sufficient for the experiment to fail?

One could argue that NORC understood what was meant by political feasibility and relevance. Clearly, NORC was learning the bureaucratic procedures for information procurement, processing, and application. As time went on, the staff even became skillful in dealing with these rules—especially those of the OMB. NORC was learning, inductively, the implicit information policies of the participating agencies and NORC's role in those policies. Moreover, NORC believed that once it was deeply embedded in an organization, it would be difficult for the organization to discontinue its participation.

Given these preliminary observations, our analysis of the next stage will begin to resolve the competing hypotheses. Do all the experimental conditions have to be met for the knowledge-transfer mechanism to be successful and for utilization to occur? Or, alternatively, is there an overriding constraint operating on the knowledge-inquiry system? That is, does the issue of control, from the perspective of the participating bureaucratic agencies, predominate?

CHAPTER 5

Assessing
the Survey Experiment

▭◖▭▭▭▭◖▭◖▭▭▭▭◖▭

In December 1973, when the grant funds for the project were expended, NORC had completed seven of the thirteen cycles originally anticipated. All actors in the experiment knew that the future of the project had to be resolved: Would CNS continue and would agencies fund the project from their own budgets? Between December 1973 and June 1974, decisions were made concerning funding, working relationships between the continuing agencies and NORC, and coordination of the agencies that wanted to continue to participate in the CNS. The actors had to decide what types of rules and procedures were appropriate and applicable to CNS, a multipurpose, multiagency knowledge-transfer mechanism.

The Funding Decision

In December 1973, the agencies participating in this experiment, including NSF and OMB, held meetings to determine the future of the project. One of the by-products of these meetings was an evaluation of the project. Initially, two of the original four agencies decided to continue to fund the survey, and only one of the three newer clients was interested in continuing the survey. After some coaxing from the two original users who decided to continue, a third agency of the original group contributed funds to support the survey.

The agencies were asked to make two decisions with respect to future funding: whether to contribute funds to finish the first year's worth of fieldwork, and whether to include the CNS as a line-budget item for the next fiscal year. The one original user that did not contribute funds to finish the first year's fieldwork said it would give separate consideration to the question of funding the project for the full fiscal year. One of the newer clients did not have budgetary funds of its own to contribute. As a result, these two departments had a discussion at the secretarial level, and both were interested in participating in the project using similar sets of questions. They agreed that the department with funds would support the project for both agencies for the six months needed to complete the first year's fieldwork, then the other department would contribute its own funds, once they were allocated by Congress, for the full fiscal year. Thus some cooperation among participants was demonstrated.

OMB and NSF played an active role in coordination meetings among the client agencies for the purpose of making these funding decisions. Since NSF was the granting agency and the full terms of the grant had not been met, it felt some responsibility for contributing to this decision. OMB took a coordinating role because it wanted the project to have a fair chance to survive. Our interviews revealed that OMB's role with respect to this project was an unusual one; the office did not usually try to take an active role in the procurement process. OMB drafted the following memo to clarify the issues related to the continuous funding of the project.

Among the issues briefly discussed at our meeting of July 18 on the NORC survey were the questions of interim financing for the survey and the arrangements that would best meet agency needs and resources, assuming continuation of the survey beyond the test period. Since continuation of the survey through the balance of fiscal year 1974 seems assured, it seems useful to proceed with the proposed meeting concerned with the longer run.

As a starting point for discussion at the meeting it would be helpful if you would seriously consider your agency's position on the following:

a. NORC desires a grant or contract with a single agency that will accept fund transfers from other agencies. Two issues are obvious: Which agency should that be? and, What are the relationships among agencies and the funding agency?

b. What is the optimal funding period beginning July 1974? It is possible that the normal federal review process would be better served if decisions were made in January or February for extension and therefore a one-year lead should be built in.

c. What are the services that an agency must or can purchase through continuous versus partial or occasional use of the survey? For example, do some agencies want only the survey with minimal NORC input regarding design and data analysis?

d. Should there be a standing capacity to allow for "visiting" users, that is, agencies which will participate infrequently?

e. What should the control and information mechanisms be among the federal participants as well as in relation to NORC?

There were also agency participants involved in this decision who had not previously been exposed to the project—agencies that thought they might want to become part of the CNS. Because of the unusual procedures followed with respect to procurement, upper-level policy makers (assistant secretary and above) in several agencies were not involved in the project prior to the funding crisis. Of the seven participating organizations, only three had experienced any upper-level involvement prior to this time. Given this crisis, however, upper-level policy makers had to become involved since they had responsibility for budgetary decisions.

In the short run, the brokers helped to gain support for the CNS. Even in those agencies that decided not to continue with the project, the brokers definitely helped the project gain serious consideration. In the long run, however, it is not clear whether the project was helped by the brokers. The interviews tend to show that when it was time to make long-term commitments, the brokers were less willing to take risks than at any other time in the development of the project. These individuals perceived that they were being identified with the project: "If I put my support on the line and the project fails, it's my hide." The brokers were willing to go to policy makers once and ask for support. However, if no other agency participants were willing to join them in making a case for support, the brokers did not feel that they could risk their positions for the CNS project.

Organizational factors were dominant in influencing the outcome of the funding decision. In the case of the one original user that decided not to continue, this phenomenon is most clearly illustrated. Two of the agency participants in other departments asked their supervising assistant secretaries to pressure the appropriate assistant secretary at this third department to fund CNS. Without this third user, CNS would have been discontinued because its funds would not been sufficient for the fieldwork. Each individual segment was essential. This third agency's decision to continue did not represent a positive evaluation of the CNS; rather, the agency was responding to pressure from the other two. For the one original agency that did not continue with the survey, the explanation for its decision also depended more on organizational phenomena than any other factor. One assistant secretary, asked to review the project, did not feel that it was serving the interests of his department. Other NORC competitors, with whom he had close relations, were doing a "far better job" in serving this function. Although other agency participants were mildly in favor of continuing with the CNS, the wishes of the assistant secretary dominated. Again, a trade-off was involved: the staff's mild desire to continue support of the survey was subordinated to organizational harmony.

The Evaluation of NORC

In analyzing these funding decisions, we must examine the criteria used by participants in judging the success of the project. Three primary questions concerned agency participants: Did CNS provide information that was relevant and useful to the agencies? Was information provided in a cost-effective manner? Was CNS filling gaps in the agency's overall information needs better than other available sources? In other words, was CNS the unique source of information that the RANN guidelines originally specified? NSF and RANN considered two additional criteria: CNS's success in meeting the terms of the project grant and the federal agencies' success in using the new information resource. OMB developed criteria from a somewhat different perspective. Like NSF, it was concerned about the federal government's performance. OMB sought to evaluate the extent to which CNS information fit the overall information needs of the federal government and the extent to which the CNS represented a unique information resource.

The federal agencies that evaluated CNS concluded that it possessed the following strengths:

1. CNS allowed agencies to take immediate advantage of an ongoing survey to meet immediate information needs.
2. CNS had the potential of fast turnaround time so that results could affect day-to-day policy formulation.
3. CNS allowed agencies to experiment with asking questions in different kinds of ways. This flexibility was not a feature of information resources available through the normal procurement channels.
4. CNS provided independent validity and collaboration to other information resources used by the government.
5. CNS provided direct inputs to policy formulation.

The agencies concluded that the project's major weaknesses were:

1. NORC did not anticipate the problems that it encountered with this project. The CNS staff should have been able to advise agencies of time delays and cost considerations before they occurred. Moreover, NORC could have been more active in advising agencies that the sampling procedures did not provide sufficiently significant results for certain kinds of questions.
2. NORC did not understand the government system.
3. The cost of the project was far too high, considering the product.
4. Certain core questions could be eliminated from the survey and reduce the costs. Those research questions were primarily of interest to NORC alone.
5. NORC should have opened a Washington office early in the project to serve the day-to-day needs of the agencies instead of relying on the agency brokers.
6. The agencies were asked to evaluate NORC services before they had sufficient data upon which to base this judgment.
7. One agency felt that NORC was not providing technically competent information.
8. Agencies did not have sufficient time available to devote to this project. Since NORC was not able to anticipate policy problems, and since it did not understand the operations of government, agencies had to devote significant staff resources if the project were to serve a useful purpose.

One agency's evaluation included the following specific comments:

1. The survey firm has made substantial investment in time, resources, and prestige in the design and initial implementation of the system. Further, the firm has been responsive to the requests and suggestions of its agency clients. All indications are that the survey results will be

technically sound and of high professional quality.
2. The turnaround time—from the date questions
   are submitted to the date survey results are received—is excessive. Though the proposal talked
   in terms of weeks and even days, we are now
   closer to five or six months. This needs to be
   drastically reduced. Two months is perhaps a
   realistic target. The time savings will have to occur at both the client and survey firm ends.
3. The survey firm needs to have more day-to-day
   interaction with its client users. The survey firm
   should consider alternative means for bringing
   this about, including the full-time or part-time
   assignment of a representative to Washington.
4. The allocation of survey time among client
   users needs to be clarified. At present, NORC
   questions occupy 50 to 60 percent of the total.
   If this is to continue, there should be some as-
   surance that NORC is assuming a proportionate
   share of the cost.
5. Additional interaction among the client users
   would help the participants make better use of
   the information being collected by other clients
   as well as help identify issues and information
   of mutual relevance. The process could be further aided by having OMB meet with the clients, perhaps chairing the group.
6. Within the department, it would simplify administrative arrangements to have one or two
   agencies having department-wide responsibilities
   take the lead in identifying issues and formulating questions.

A second agency evaluation stated:

Our experience with the survey has been
very favorable. It is exactly the kind of vehicle
which an institution dedicated to a great deal of in-
house research requires. Many of the questions
which we investigate are too narrow-gauge to justi-

fy the mounting of complete surveys. We have many small questions to investigate, too many to make issuing discrete Requests for Proposal (RFPs) on each topic workable. The NORC Survey permitted us to do small studies at reasonable costs in both money and staff time.

So much for the suitability of the basic concept to our needs. The next topic is the technical value of this particular survey and the quality of our experience with the NORC staff. I have had an immensely positive relationship with the NORC consultants. Many of us on the staff are very familiar with survey research. Yet, all of us are convinced that the survey work done for us by NORC is vastly better both in conceptualization and design than it would have been had we relied on our own resources. The fact that we have found the technical interaction with NORC staff rewarding does not mean that it has always been easy. None of us likes to submit to probing questions about why we are advocating particular design features in a study. Sometimes that has led to temporary prickly relationships between researchers here and people on the NORC staff. That, however, is in the nature of the relationship between one researcher and another and can be avoided only at the cost of lower technical quality of the work. I think all of us have profited from our interaction with the NORC staff, and wouldn't have had it any other way.

Data analysis on survey results sometimes has been slower than we and NORC would have liked, and that may count as a minor disappointment. But NORC has generally been prompt in providing the tabulations we have requested. As an example of the results obtained, I am enclosing my own paper on goals for education. All of the statistics were computed at my direction by the NORC staff. We have now obtained tapes and codebooks for the first few cycles and can do our own analysis. But we expect to continue using NORC's data processing services, at least for part of our work.

As an overall evaluation, the fact that we added money to the initial NSF grant and are now preparing to add considerably more money to the contract for continuing the survey speaks for itself. It has been indispensable to us.

A final comment is about the problems which we have experienced and observed in coordinating a government agency's use of a resource like the NORC survey. It wasn't very hard because a lot of other people and I found our self-interest being served by an orderly use of the survey. We had no problem in assuring its use and in developing a queue of potential users. However, I think that other agencies may have had considerable trouble ensuring continuity in the use of the survey. That I think is something that NSF, as an agency bridging the gap between research institutions and the government, should try to take into account in the future when it provides such juicy but hard-to-use resources to government agencies. In all, I think your grant to NORC was a major public service and hope you will fund other analogous general research vehicles in the future.

Overall, the agencies were most disturbed by being asked to evaluate the usefulness of the project without having the information upon which to base this decision. One participant said, "On the basis of what we had, we had to make a negative judgment; if we had had more information given to us, in terms of written reports submitted by NORC, it may have changed the picture." Even the agencies that decided to continue to fund NORC were annoyed with its administrative incompetence. Some agencies were also disturbed by the fact that they did not perceive CNS as a unique source of information: it did not provide fast turnaround time and it did not speak to the short-term policy needs of these agencies.

Within the agencies in which CNS was most popular, there was disagreement about the criteria of policy relevance and fast turnaround time. However, these agencies were also not convinced that CNS represented a unique source of information. They wanted to continue with it primarily because it was organizationally convenient: "It is here and we can use it now and not have to go through the long and difficult procurement procedure. It is not that another survey may not be able to provide the same information or even be able to provide it more efficiently."

Let us note that NORC's technical capabilities were not being questioned by the vast majority of participants; they were assumed. Neither was the utility of survey research for the purposes of policy making being challenged. The agencies' questions concerned the utility of this particular instrument, the ease with which it could be used, and the problems involved in coordinating it. The most important short-term criteria were utility and ease; in the long run, the coordination problem was dominant.

From NSF's perspective, the greatest strengths of the CNS were its ability to attract agency commitments, its ability to speak to policy-relevant needs, and the working relationships it established with some agencies. NSF's greatest reservations were related to the cost overrun, NORC's lack of understanding of policy issues facing agencies, NORC's inflexibility in staffing the project, and the tensions between NORC and RANN concerning the central theme for the project agreed upon in the proposal.

Specifically, one NSF member offered the following evaluation in a memo: "I noted that NORC had been able to complete only about one half the survey work for which the NSF award had been made. _____ [agency] decided to terminate a contract with NORC for a large-scale study of family growth. The overrun with _____ [project] was approximately $750,000. _____ [agency] has decided to have the data processing done by another contractor. Among the problems of NORC identified by _____ [agency] were: comparatively low response rates; difficulties in establishing satisfactory cost estimates; difficulties in establishing and maintaining quality control; comparatively heavy staff turnover; and some difficulty in assigning sufficient manpower to supervise fieldwork operations."

From OMB's perspective, CNS' greatest asset was the uniqueness of the methodological instrument and its capabilities. OMB perceived CNS's greatest weaknesses to be related to the cost overruns and to its inability to solve the coordination problems.

Our interviews on agency evaluation focused on three variables: the ways in which staff relationships with NORC differed from standard relations between contractors and the agencies; whether CNS data were applied to problems for which other research had not been used; and whether the way in which decisions were made concerning the CNS was special, unusual, or unique. It was imperative to determine how the experimental nature of the project affected decisions about the procurement procedure. The answer to this last question, in particular, certainly affects the generalizability of our findings.

From interviewing participants during the planning stage, we learned that policy makers were not as involved in the initial decisions as they would have been with other information resources. The researchers had more influence on decisions concerning this project than they would have had in the normal procurement process. Thus, NORC had an obstacle to overcome. Researchers did not usually procure information by themselves unless they were drawing on the literature or were able to acquire information without expense to the agency. But in this case, the policy makers would eventually have to make a decision concerning agency budgetary commitments. For an information resource competing for agency funds, CNS's development, in the early stages, was rather unique. Of course, this experimental aspect was one of the reasons RANN decided to fund CNS.

However, as CNS succeeded in diversifying, the staff arrangements could no longer be considered unique. Policy makers became involved as much as they were in any survey research. In some cases, the staff had spent less time with the project than they would have with regular contractors. This, too, changed when agencies began to commit their own funds to the project. When budgetary decisions were made, CNS was submitted to the same kind of evaluation as other contractors for survey research.

Regarding the kinds of problems to which CNS information was being applied, participants reported that the information they requested was applied to the same kind of policy problems that other survey data were. Originally, some participants were motivated to become involved in the project so they could use it in a way that other research had not been used in the past. However, these expectations were, as a whole, not realized. In only two cases was this principle applied; then, for only one cycle's worth of questions. In other words, the CNS was not considered as a unique source of information. Thus, CNS can be compared with other surveys concerning the quality of information, the optimal use of the information, the policy areas information was applied to, and the usefulness and effectiveness of the information. In terms of evaluation criteria, CNS is unique only in terms of the design of the administrative structure of the project, that is, multiagency coordination.

Thus there is a comparative data base upon which we can draw in evaluating decisions concerning budgetary commitments, the quality of the information resource, and the agency's decisions to continue to receive a particular kind of information. This comparative analysis is best illustrated by an evaluation of the information applied to the energy-related policy areas. Agency participants indicated that other surveys could have provided the same information, but because CNS was operating, it was used.

In interviews, respondents were asked to specifically compare their experiences with CNS and their experiences with other contractors. In addition, they were asked to compare the criteria they used to judge this project with the ones they used to judge other research of this kind. The criteria applied to decisions of what information to collect, how to apply it, and how to judge it are not unique to this project.

Coordination and Diversification

After some pressure from all other participants in the experiment, NSF agreed to continue to coordinate the short-term funding of the project. In other words, the agencies would funnel their funds through a mechanism set up by NSF and RANN.

However, once the project was no longer receiving grant funds, some other arrangement for coordinating the funding had to be made if the project was to continue its field operations.

Thus, from the time that the grant funds ran out, the project faced a continuing funding crisis. Six months' worth of support was allocated by the three agencies. (One of these three was committing funds for a second agency as well; there were, therefore, four participants.) They only postponed the long-term problem. The participants saw several options open to them: NSF or RANN could continue to serve as the lead agency with the responsibility for coordinating funding; OMB could assume the role of coordinating; one of the participating agencies could assume the lead role; each agency could write a separate contract with NORC; or NSF could agree to grant additional money for the project's survival.

At first, all the participants in the project except NSF favored the last option. Many agency participants, including OMB, argued that NSF had not given the project a fair chance. Furthermore, these participants argued that NSF had not taken into consideration budgetary cycles and government procedures with respect to budgetary allocations. They said that NSF would be responsible for the termination of the project because government regulations would not allow the agencies to add the project to their budgets at such a late date. NSF argued that it was not its responsibility to worry about budgetary processes; this, too, was to be worked out between the agencies and NORC. However, because of some NSF interest in the energy-related areas, NSF seemed willing at one point to provide the majority of the support necessary for the project's continuation. As a result, RANN convened a meeting to discuss this possibility with agency participants. At this meeting, however, RANN withdrew its support because the agencies could not articulate the specific uses they would make of this project. NSF felt that such specificity was a necessary condition for the continuation of the project, that it would not be fulfilling its institutional mission if it did not insist on this criterion. NSF feared that it could be held accountable to Congress for such actions and was unwilling to threaten its organizational position.

After NSF's withdrawal, some agency participants turned to OMB for coordination. OMB said that although it wanted to see the project continue it was not an appropriate coordinator. Toward the end of this period, however, OMB suggested that it might be willing to coordinate the project as part of an overall planning effort by the government. Agency participants were not enthusiastic about this possibility. They already resented "too much OMB control." Sensing the agency resistance and noting the lengthiness of the planning effort, OMB concluded that it could not coordinate the project.

Thus, it was left to the agencies interested in continuing with the CNS to find some solution. Bureaucratic rules would not allow them to write separate contracts with NORC. Any separate contract would have to stipulate specific services to be delivered over a specific period of time. Such stipulations would contradict the multiagency design of the project. Bureaucratic rules required multiagency projects to have an overall carrier or lead agency. When one agency expressed interest in serving this lead role, other agencies again raised questions about who would control the information and how one agency could truly represent the others. Then the agency's secretary decided that it was inappropriate for his agency to take the lead role. As a result, the CNS went out of the field in June 1974.

The problem of coordination could have been avoided had the original agreements among agencies (reached at the time of the original funding crisis) been realized. During that stage of the project, energy concerns became central to the project. One original departmental user was willing to pay two thirds of the $750,000 needed for the short-term continuation of the project on the basis of an agreement made at the secretarial level. Once the money was allocated to the second department, it would take over the primary responsibility for coordination of this project. This agreement would have solved the coordination problem: The agency contributing the most money for the continuation of the project would have coordinated it. However, this agreement was not honored. At the assistant secretary's level, the second agency had close ties to one of NORC's competitors. This second agency recommended that a general Request for Proposal (RFP) be sent out and all survey research organizations be allowed to bid on it. As a result, the first agency decided that it was no longer advantageous for it to carry the burden for the joint project. Although it considered CNS a valuable resource and had shown its good faith, it did not want to risk being the sole supporter of the project in the long run. Even the strongest supporters of CNS within this agency felt that some review was necessary. After some reflection by the other agencies, while CNS was not in the field, they were to decide whether to support the concept of a continuous national survey, one administered by NORC or some other plan.

Among the agencies that continued to support the project, participation was limited to the policy areas already developed. A few new policy areas in energy were introduced, and other agencies narrowed their focus: fewer substantive concerns and less staff participation. As the coordination problems became greater, participation became less frequent. With the exception of the energy-related policy areas, there was no upper-level policy involvement in the project. In the energy areas, upper-level involvement became more intense and frequent with respect to reviewing NORC's results; however, questionnaire formulation was not focused upon.

The coordination problems and associated concerns about who should control the information are the most important components of this stage of the project's development. The project was designed to allow agencies to share the information base composed of all the questions asked over the history of the project. Many agencies were concerned that the coordinator might also control the information resources. More importantly, the coordination problem illustrates the importance of establishing orderly bureaucratic procedures and the saliency of individual organizational concerns.

This finding would suggest that the importance or relevance of survey research was not at stake during this evaluative phase. If this were the case, agencies would reject survey research in general. But our interviews indicate that survey research results are valued by the federal government and used in the formulation of policy. As the study by Caplan and others (1975) shows, survey research is one of the most valued data collection instruments at the federal level.

Given the value attached to this kind of information, control and management become all the more important. If an agency finds an information resource valuable, then it wants to be able to control it and coordinate it. If an agency cannot possess this capability for one instrument, it will logically employ one with the same technical capabilities that it can control. Indeed, three pieces of independent evidence confirm our conclusion that these organizational phenomena were operative during the development of the CNS. First, those agencies that initially dropped out of the project had already employed another survey research resource to address the same policy questions for which the CNS had been used. Second, agencies used the concept of a continuous survey in writing new RFPs and in negotiating with new contractors. Indeed, three of the four agencies that dropped out of the project wrote RFPs requesting the same type of information. NORC was even invited to bid on them.

Third, consistent with the release of the RFPs during the evaluation process, the agency participants interviewed noted that they wanted to continue to receive the kind of information provided by the CNS even if this one particular project were discontinued. In one memo, written at the secretarial level between two agencies involved with the CNS, this judgment is confirmed: "We believe that such surveys should continue as long as the energy 'crisis' does. Their value is recognized by those in the department and the [officials] who read their results. [The secretary] considers the survey worthwhile, although he doubts the validity of the regional differentiation in view of the small size of the sample. He would seek alternate survey data if the NORC survey ends."

Furthermore, some agency participants discussed the conceptual framework of the CNS at meetings between agencies and at international meetings. If agencies challenged the quality of the survey information or the conceptual framework, they would not have taken actions to revive these concepts for operational purposes or invited NORC to continue to be part of their knowledge-inquiry system.

During the six months between December 1973 and June 1974, each agency had to decide whether to commit long-term funding to CNS. As already indicated, several agencies were willing to fund CNS if appropriate bureaucratic arrangements, acceptable to all participating actors, could have been formulated. The organizational problems were not resolved, however, despite the willingness of one of the participating agencies to take the lead in coordinating the continuation of the CNS project. Thus, in June 1974, the CNS went out of the field. None of the participating agencies allocated long-term funding to the project.

The agencies maintained some contact with the CNS staff during this period because data analysis was still being performed. Agencies were still receiving information and deciding whether to use it.

The Relationship between NORC and the Agencies. NORC's contact with the agencies during this phase was basically limited to the original brokers. NORC sent results to them, and they were responsible for distributing the information to the appropriate agency participants. Policy makers were involved in this stage of development only to the extent that the information was utilized by them. (See Chapter Six for a fuller discussion of utilization.) The contacts with staff members were limited to occasional long-distance telephone calls. OMB had no contact with the project, and NSF had limited contact to arrange for a final report to be submitted to it.

The energy-related policy areas again served as the exception to the rule. NORC had more frequent contacts with staff research personnel in these policy areas to complete written reports for the agencies, for the public, and for publication. The CNS staff also attended some meetings with these federal representatives to discuss the results of these data. Arrangements were also made for NORC to do some limited survey work for some of these participants in the energy area.

Retrospective Evaluation. As the final analysis reports were being written by NORC, we conducted interviews with participants in the project. They were asked to assess the project's success, to evaluate the strengths and weaknesses of the project, and to state whether they would have liked to have seen CNS in the field at that time.

The majority of the participants felt that the project was a "limited success." Even the most critical participants felt that some "marginal progress" had been achieved in reaching the project's original objectives. Participants noted that the agencies had learned to use national survey information, that information was transmitted to people who could act upon it, and that some good working relationships developed between researchers and policy makers.

In those agencies that described CNS's success as only marginal, staff explained that their agencies had not learned how to use this valuable information resource. One agency was experiencing a shift of administration when NORC was developing the project, and another agency was undergoing careful congressional scrutiny. In both cases, agency participants felt that they were unable to devote the necessary time to the development of the project. They stated that NORC had not been given a real chance to succeed, because of external pressures.

Two significant points were highlighted in the interviews: the importance of the energy crisis to the project and the insufficiency of attention given to the rules and procedures of the federal government in previous assessments of the project. Several participants observed that had it not been for the energy crisis CNS would have folded once the original grant funds were depleted. In making this argument, they noted that only in energy policy areas had the project been used for the purposes for which it was designed—upper-level policy makers utilizing public opinion data. Also, exclusively in the energy areas did upper-level policy makers have any consistent and intensive involvement in the project. In characterizing this development, one participant said, "My major reservation about this project is that I wish the energy panic never happened. If it hadn't come in, we probably would have gotten a lot more solid research done"; another observed, "Because of the energy crisis this project could not be given a fair test." It is difficult to assess the validity of this argument. Certainly, CNS was not designed for the purpose of being responsive to a crisis in public policy formulation. However, RANN did intend to design an information resource capable of meeting the immediate needs of policy makers. One could argue that the energy crisis was merely a fair test of whether the research instrument was capable of responding to the immediate needs of policy makers. But other components and capabilities of the project's design were probably not given a fair test because the immediacy of the energy crisis required NORC's concentration. The CNS happened to be at the right place at the right time. It was an ongoing research instrument that energy policy makers could easily take advantage of to ensure fast results. NORC became preoccupied with energy policy areas because it perceived them as critical to its survival and continued funding. To this extent, the crisis undoubtedly constrained the experimental nature of the project. When the crisis waned, the need for the CNS waned with it. Had the project been more diversified within other agencies, the end of the energy crisis would not necessarily have meant the end of the project.

Participants also echoed NSF's and OMB's position: The federal government was as much at fault for the success or failure of the project as NORC was. In retrospect, the agency participants were able to admit the weaknesses of their own approach. However, this realization did not lead the agencies to state that they wished CNS were still in the field. Most participants felt that were CNS functioning, it would experience the same coordination problems that caused it to falter. Others thought that the federal government would make the same mistakes with the project as it had in the past. However, two of the original participants wished the project were in the field so that it could be used for its intended purposes. One even specified policy areas to which it could be applied.

Respondents were also asked: "What would you change with the CNS if you could start over again?" Their answers reflected the shortcomings and weaknesses they recited in evaluating this project; for example, a Washington office should have been opened early in the project, NORC should have established contacts with the secretary's office from the project's inception and developed a more realistic budget.

Discussion and Analysis: The Success of the CNS

As noted at the beginning of Chapter Four, the most interesting parts of the CNS experiment are those that help us learn about knowledge-inquiry systems in the context of applied research at the federal level. Moreover, from the perspective of RANN, it is important to assess the extent to which this experiment was successful. At this stage, success can be measured only in terms of the success of the knowledge-transfer mechanism.

The Experimental Conditions—Competing Hypotheses. At the end of Chapter Four, we formulated a preliminary conclusion: the success of a knowledge-transfer mechanism (such as the CNS) is not dependent upon meeting each of the experimental conditions related to bridging the two cultures. However, this conclusion needs to be qualified. With the exception of cost, NORC met all the experimental conditions for some of the agencies—especially for those dealing with energy-related policy issues. Even with the other participating agencies, most of the conditions were met to the satisfaction of the participants. The National Institute of Education, for example, obtained the information it requested in time for an important decision concerning the commitment of long-term funds, even though the data were not transmitted within the three to four weeks originally specified in the grant.

But, more importantly, agencies did not make their final decisions about committing funds to CNS on the basis of the extent to which NORC met *all* the criteria presumed to be related to underutilization of social science knowledge. Instead, the decisions were almost exclusively based on bureaucratic criteria. Agencies do not, as a rule, want to share information with officials from other agencies; the rules governing CNS, supported by OMB, allowed—even encouraged—the sharing of information resources. Similarly, most bureaucrats do not want to share control and ownership over information resources; yet, CNS required them to do this in two different ways—agencies were to pool questions in policy areas that interested more than one agency and each agency had access to the others' information. The design of the CNS almost required agencies to continue to cooperate if the project was to be an enduring one. Despite the demonstrated utility of the results generated by the survey and the convenience of access to data of this kind, the organizational traditions and the importance assigned to control and ownership far outweighed any attraction to the CNS.

From the perspective of the bureaucratization of the knowledge-inquiry system, NSF built failure into the design of this experiment by requiring cooperation, coordination, and the sharing of resources. It is not that cooperation never occurs in federal agencies; but it cannot be forced on agencies by the design of a particular program.

NORC was, however, successful in gaining intraorganizational cooperation and, to some limited extent (in the energy-related areas), temporary interorganizational cooperation. They could not overcome the agencies' resistance to sharing the information and relinquishing full control over their own knowledge-inquiry system.

The Bureaucratization of the Knowledge-Inquiry System. These results point to the bureaucratization of the knowledge-inquiry system within federal agencies. Cost, timeliness, relevance, and the like are necessary but not sufficient conditions for the success of an experimental knowledge-transfer mechanism. Issues of control and adherence to established organizational procedures have to be resolved before such an experiment could have a chance to be successful.

Besides the events already discussed, others point to the accuracy of this statement. First, all the agencies that discontinued their participation in the experiment either had arranged for a substitute (competitor to NORC in survey research) or were prepared to use regular procurement channels to locate one. It is significant that they were willing to use regular procurement channels, which require a substantial commitment of time and staff resources. Their recourse to such processes points to the unacceptability of the bureaucratic arrangements associated with the CNS. The CNS was not discontinued because a judgment was made concerning the quality of survey research in general or its applicability to policy problems in specific. Had these been the agencies' judgments, they would not have continued seeking to contract for future continuous surveys.

Second, related to issues of control, *trust* is more important than *quality* or *objectivity* of information. An operating principle in government seems to be that new resources and tools must prove themselves worthy of trust. Agencies take a detached and skeptical attitude during the time they are establishing this trust. Thus, agencies rely more on other government agencies for guidance than the outsiders trying to introduce a new resource. This pattern is pervasive even when the new tool is introduced with government funds. NSF's position caused confusion during the funding period that was only compounded during the planning stage. Especially in a situation in which agencies are already cautious, they will not take risks if the consequences are not fully clear. Whether or not one judges NSF's position as a good one, clearly it resulted in greater detachment on the part of some agency participants. The agencies perceived the risks involved in becoming closer to NORC as greater than any tangible benefits. For the purposes of experimentation, NSF was undoubtedly taking a scientifically correct position. However, in terms of bureaucratic procedures, RANN should have realized that skepticism with respect to this kind of information resource and resistance to current procurement procedures could not be overcome by a project whose design did not recognize these rules. Thus, during the planning stage, NORC was not successful in achieving a goal essential to the optimal operation of the project: proving itself to the agencies so that participants would feel NORC could be trusted.

To some extent, NORC was the victim of a catch-22 bind. The CNS staff could not be trusted if "they did not prove themselves by showing that they understood agency problems." Yet, it is impossible to prove oneself without agency cooperation. The agency participants were unrealistic in their judgment that the experiment would not require them to educate NORC. It is just this kind of interaction that has the potential to begin to bridge the two cultures. However, inflexible positions on both sides resulted in reinforcing the gap between researchers and policy makers.

Third, agency participants felt that they were in the difficult position of having to make trade-offs to reach decisions concerning the future of CNS. Despite any interest or commitment to CNS, the participants were not willing to risk their organizational status or position to continue to support one particular project. These kinds of trade-offs were involved in the brokers' decisions concerning how to define their role in the project, their decisions during the agency evaluation of CNS, and upper-level policy makers' decisions related to the coordination problems faced by CNS.

Other Measures of Success. Another perspective on success might be that the bureaucratization of the knowledge-inquiry system points to a partial success for CNS; even though it did not succeed in institutionalizing itself, it did a lot to legitimize the use of survey research in the federal government. Even the critics of CNS recognized the utility of the survey instrument in helping them solve policy-relevant problems.

Considering the staff and budget resources devoted to this one project, survey research is potentially of great importance to policy makers. At least, one must conclude, policy makers seek the opportunity to have these resources at their disposal. (Factors that affect subsequent use of this information are discussed in Chapter Six.) This case study also suggests that resources are not allocated to produce the greatest amount of information. Agencies contract for different studies to speak to the same policy problems. Decision makers seek collaboration and validation; this method allows them to choose which study is most useful to them. In other words, sources that provide unique information are not valued as much as those which can be collaborated. This desire for validation helps to account for the vast amount of information that agencies collect. The CNS study demonstrates how social science information can be made a relevant resource in the eyes of policy makers. Even though concerns over utilization and policy relevance possessed great currency in the federal government, they were not well defined by those talking about their importance. However, one should not conclude that information collection is related exclusively to direct plans for utilization. Although information is collected with distinct uses in mind, the final results may not be used in the intended manner (see Chapter Six for a full discussion of this matter). Similarly, a decision concerning whether particular information is to be collected may be independent of decisions concerning its immediate relevance or utilization.

Relationships in the Knowledge-Inquiry System. Beyond assessing the success of the CNS, our analysis should shed light on the development of information policies within federal agencies. Regarding relationships between researchers and users, for example, several lessons were learned: Client-contractor relationships should be clearly defined from the inception of the project, and regular procurement procedures should be followed even if agencies are not committing funds during the initial phases of the project. It is also true that there is no substitute for the strong involvement of upper-level policy makers; they should not be replaced by brokers. With respect to introducing and evaluating a new information resource, staff members are expected to be objective assessors of its value. This is especially true of research agencies that continuously have to choose among several information resources. Moreover, to whatever extent possible, some kind of broad consensus should be reached before evaluating an information resource. Within this context, the broker role had profound effects on the development of the project. To the extent that the brokers were seen as advocates, their opinion was not valued. To the extent that communications were funneled through them, a broad consensus could not be reached because other staff members did not have sufficient exposure to the project. One could, however, argue that given the communications gap between bureaucrats and researchers, someone within an agency has to take responsibility for introducing an experiment of this kind if it is to have any chance of being recognized as useful and diversified. It should be a concern of all parties to fully understand the objectives of a research project.

Beyond the potential tensions created by this broker role, some actual tensions did emerge between the agencies and NORC. From the agencies' perspective, the lengthiness of the planning stage resulted in the loss of some interest in the project. This was especially true of higher-level participants outside the research departments, who had many other information resources to occupy their attention. Again, in terms of bureaucratic procedures, the time delay was more important than the explanation for it. Obviously, the agencies' lack of precision in defining their interests contributed to the problem. However, it is not in the interest of an agency's organizational mission to devote time to a project that has not yet proven itself. Moreover, this experience helps only to confirm operating assumptions with respect to social science information: It is hard to acquire, it takes a long time to acquire, and it cannot, therefore, meet short-term policy needs.

NSF was explicitly interested in discovering whether survey research could be used for policy-making purposes and whether it could become institutionalized in agency budgets. Implicitly, however, this experiment was also a test of the operations of the federal government. Would bureaucratic procedures be flexible enough to allow a fair test of the project? As already suggested, the planning stage created some tension over this important question. If the federal agencies did not perceive that their own ways of operation were also being tested, then the experiment would be one-sided, with the burden of proof put exclusively on the producers of the information. The brokers recognized that the federal government was being tested as much as the producers of knowledge; but other staff participants realized this significantly less. This provides further evidence that the brokers may not have been doing NORC a service in that they were not representative of the agencies' expectations.

When the user organization is not the same as the funding organization, it is essential that the administrative arrangements —division of responsibility and coordination—are clear at the beginning of the project. These were left vague during the funding stage of the CNS, and this vagueness continued to plague the project throughout its twenty-four-month history.

Finally, it is equally important that when the user agency is not the funding agency, responsibilities and duties as they apply to the contractor or grantee must be mutually understood and accepted. There is no doubt that, in keeping its role vague, NSF negatively affected the development of the experiment.

Overall, however, it is fair to conclude that the experimental conditions for the CNS project were given a fair and adequate test. It is one of the few administrative quasi-experiments conducted over the last decade that can be evaluated. In some cases, all the conditions were met; in others, they were not. However, in no case were these the overriding factors in determining the success of the CNS as an experimental knowledge-transfer mechanism.

CHAPTER 6

Utilization
of the Survey
Information

So far we have evaluated the CNS experiment exclusively on the basis of the success of the knowledge-transfer mechanism. Which of the competing hypotheses concerning success seemed most valid? Would such an experiment work in the future? If so, under what conditions? In terms of these experimental conditions, only the "if" part of an "if/then" statement has been completed. The two cultures theory hypothesizes that utilization should automatically follow if the knowledge transfer mechanism has successfully been implemented. In this chapter we analyze the patterns of utilization of the information generated through the CNS. Specifically, the analysis focuses on differences in patterns of utilization across policy areas and at different levels of the decision-making hierarchy. Selective patterns of utilization are also examined.

The case history of the CNS points to several findings that are pursued in this chapter. Agency personnel are required to justify requests to collect new information in terms of the policy problems to which it will be applied. Thus, we need to ask the question, To what extent are these specifically defined expectations concerning use realized? In this same context, we also discovered that program agencies have more difficulty in defining these specific issues than policy makers. We will pursue this point, too, in terms of patterns of actual utilization.

We followed a two-step process in analyzing the patterns of utilization. First, the flows of information were traced from the time that a full NORC report was submitted to the agencies until the time that the information was not passed on to another person within the agency. Basically, this portion of the analysis concerns the dissemination of information. That a particular staff member simply receives a letter, memo, or a copy of the full report sent by NORC does not necessarily imply that it will be put to a specific use.

Second, using the policy area as the basic unit of analysis (as outlined in Chapter Two), we analyze the kinds and types of uses for the CNS data; for example, briefing an assistant secretary, writing a memo to a superior, or writing a journal article or paper. *Use,* or *utilization,* refers specifically to the entrance of information in the policy-making process. Information comes to the desk of a decision maker (mere dissemination), he reads it, and it influences the discussion of policy. This potential of influencing a decision is the critical component of our definition of utilization within policy making. As part of this analysis, we compare different policy areas, methods of question formulation, and backgrounds of users, and the extent to which original expectations with respect to use were met.

Third, combining the first two methods, we examine selective utilization of the CNS information, the form in which information was sent on, what was left out, and why. The analysis focuses on the form in which the information was sent on (a memo, a full report) and the reasons certain kinds of information were selected over others. Finally, we examine the perceptions of the respondents concerning the most important factors in understanding the utilization of information. This part of the analysis focuses on differences between users and nonusers of information. The respondents were asked to compare the uses they made of the CNS information with other social science information, in-house generated information, and information from popular journals and newspapers in the same policy areas to which CNS was applied.

Although these questions concerning utilization are straightforward, the selection of methods appropriate for purposes of analysis is not. As suggested in Chapter Two, previous studies do not clearly define utilization. In this examination, dissemination and use of information are deliberately differentiated. For most of the analysis, the policy area is used as the basic unit of analysis. In distinguishing different levels of the decision-making hierarchy, we use the individual respondents as the basic unit of analysis. In the latter case, the role of the individual is critical; in the former, the role of a piece of information and its flow through the decision-making hierarchy are critical.

The categories used in the analysis result from subjective judgments made on the basis of the longitudinal interviews conducted with respondents in this study. This is especially true for the categories of reasons for selectivity and for general use. In each case that required a subjective judgment, collaborating evidence is also provided that supports this decision—either illustrations of specific citations from the interviews or other documentation. For example, in Chapter Five we argued that the problems of coordination were related more to organizational factors than to any others. This conclusion definitely involved a judgment based on an interpretation of the data. In making this argument, however, we cited collaborating evidence: that individual agencies were using standard procurement procedures to contract for continuous national survey data. In this portion of the analysis, comparable evidence is provided to support subjective judgments.

Nevertheless, unlike a large study based on a national random sample, this study does not allow for judgments that could be considered statistically significant. Only thirty-eight respondents were interviewed, fourteen of whom were interviewed on a continuous basis. By statistical standards for evidence, therefore, our results are only suggestive and do not claim to be anything more. They represent an initial effort in an area in which empirical research has been limited.

Beyond the problems already outlined, studies of utilization face two other major methodological problems. One is the difficulty involved in making any causal inferences, even when the data base is large enough to yield statistically significant results. Statistical methods require one to isolate all the major factors contributing to the variance before such an analysis can be completed. Thus one must conceptualize the variables or factors and translate them into empirically testable propositions. In the case of policy making, one is faced with the problem of trying to conceptualize processes and styles of problem solving —both of which have diverse roots that have not been traced or operationalized and, more importantly, put in the form of empirically testable propositions. Thus, one would have to try, as we are attempting in this study, to develop these propositions. After this step is completed, it is possible to field a large-scale study to test the propositions. The difficulty involved in measuring ongoing problem solving further complicates the methodological problem.

Previous studies in this area either provide an analysis of utilization at one point in time or summarize a particular case history. The case histories tend to take the form of a postaudit: retrospective explanations of a case history. Our research tries to develop a different methodology. Although it takes the form of a case history, it is not a postaudit in that the analysis reflects the nature of an *ongoing* process. Thus, participants involved in this project were interviewed at six different times. The project was analyzed as it unfolded and developed. Groups of respondents were interviewed as they became involved in a new stage of the project's development. Thus, while our research has the limitation of lacking statistical replicability, it offers a method for analyzing live, ongoing problem solving. The data base for our analysis of utilization consists of longitudinal interviews and the documentation (letters, memos, and reports) provided by agency participants. Thirty-eight agency participants (including the staffs of OMB and NSF) were involved in decisions concerning utilization. As mentioned in Chapter Four, the most active participants were those who acted as brokers.

The second methodological problem results from the fact that utilization tends to take place in clusters. Single reports are typically not used or applied in themselves. Staff members accumulate evidence concerning a particular policy problem, summarize it, and send a report based on the compiled evidence to a policy maker. This process makes it especially difficult to trace the influence or impact of a particular piece of information. Very seldom can a policy maker point to a particular study that had a definite influence upon a decision. Often, memos do not distinguish between the various studies that informed the paper received by a policy maker. If a study is cited, it is usually mentioned in the context of several other studies. The researcher who would trace utilization, therefore, must extrapolate from the evidence provided. For example, in one policy area investigated through the use of the CNS, a memo was written that used the survey data as one resource among others. (See Appendix D for the text of the memo.) If the memo, as a whole, had an influence, then one must assume that each contributing study had an influence.

This particular problem also serves to illustrate the more general problem of measuring impact. Seldom does a final report from a cabinet meeting, a legislative proposal, or program guidelines directly draw upon and quote an empirical study. However, this kind of impact represents the only truly objective criterion for the measurement of impact. In this study, for example, there are only two instances of utilization that cite the original NORC report as part of the final product drafted on the policy problem to which the CNS was applied. If one counted only these two instances as illustrating impact, one would be ignoring many more instances in which CNS data were applied in a more indirect, untraceable fashion. Thus, we rely on judgments based on the interviews. Respondents were questioned concerning the uses made of the information collected in each policy area that they were working on. When influence was mentioned, the interviewer probed so as to be able to code the most specific category of utilization. However, there is no doubt that influence is a vague and imprecise phenomenon. But to apply stringent objective criteria would be to sacrifice the accuracy of respondents' descriptions of the information's use to them. In each instance, as much written documentation as possible was also collected. If a memo was written, the interviewer requested access to it. In this way, it was possible to make judgments about the criteria used for selectivity in reporting the information generated by CNS. This overall methodological approach is experimental in nature; there is no doubt that its validity and generalizability are yet to be proven through its application in other studies.

Basic Characteristics of the CNS Information

Before analyzing the utilization and selective utilization of the information, let us describe the basic characteristics of that information. The seven domestic service agencies involved in the project collected information for twenty-six policy areas over the eighteen months CNS was in the field. Six of these areas were of concern to more than one agency; these agencies had the opportunity to coordinate their use of the information. Thus, in our analysis of utilization, we see that there are some policy areas in which the same information was used in different ways because different agencies made different decisions concerning utilization. Moreover, any one piece of information may have been put to multiple uses by the same agency. Thus, the twenty-six policy areas may yield as many as thirty-five or forty different kinds of applications (for example, uses, questions asked, and level of policy to which the questions are aimed).

Generally, the questions asked on the CNS were to be used in either programmatic or upper-level policy areas. The expected uses were about evenly divided between programmatic and policy concerns. Approximately 97 percent of the questions asked (based on an analysis of the policy areas) were aimed at the concerns of policy makers as opposed to the individual concerns of lower-level bureaucrats. The policy makers had either been consulted in the drafting of the questions or those drafting questions knew, from staff meetings, the problems under consideration by them. In about half the cases, the policy makers were directly consulted in the writing of the questions, and in the other cases some indirect consultation, of the kind described above, was involved. In only two cases were the formulated questions of no concern to the policy makers.

In Chapter Four, we divided the questions asked through the CNS into three general categories: monitoring questions; "hot-issue" questions, which are aimed at the immediate needs of policy makers; methodological questions, which are aimed at measuring behavior or attitudes over time. Over the eighteen months that the experiment was in the field, 64.7 percent of the questions asked were of the monitoring variety, 29.4 percent of the "hot issue" variety, and approximately 5.9 percent of the methodological variety. Another way of categorizing the questions asked is: attitudinal, evaluative, and social inventory or factual questions. The social inventory and evaluative questions were asked far more often than the attitudinal ones. Approximately 47 percent of the questions were social inventory or factual, 44 percent of the evaluative variety, and 9 percent of the questions focused on public attitudes.

Patterns of Utilization

It seems natural to expect very high levels of utilization of CNS information because it was collected for specific uses and policy makers were consulted, directly or indirectly, in the vast majority of the policy areas to which this information was to be applied. However, actual utilization did not correlate well with expected uses. First, we counted forty-four uses that were expected for the information collected during the eighteen months of CNS fieldwork. In only sixteen of these forty-four cases were the expectations actually realized; in another eight cases, participants still planned to fulfill their initial expectations (see Table 2). The initial expectations were met in 73.3 percent of the cases for the policy areas and in only 16.6 percent of the cases in the program areas. This reflects the fact that

Table 2. Expected Uses (Multiple Responses Are Possible;
by Policy Area; $N = 26$)

Kinds of Uses	Expected	Realized	Planned
Program regulations	13	2	3
Program formulation	12	2	2
Policy input, upper level	15	11	0
General background	0	0	0
Future program or policy	4	1	3

the expected uses from the general policy questions were better defined than those related to programmatic concerns, and were realized far more in the energy policy areas than in any others. These results do not, however, reflect the uses other than those expected.

On the basis of the interviews, we constructed aggregate categories to describe types of utilization. After NORC reports were received by the participating agencies, each respondent was asked to report the use made of the information related to each policy area. Thus, over time we traced the different kinds of uses made of information within a particular policy area. Information gleaned in these interviews was used to construct the categories employed in this chapter. Typically, three kinds of responses were given. First, "No particular use was made of the information." When this response was given, the interviewer continued to ask about the information over time. In some cases, the response changed, and in others the information continued to be rejected. In other cases, respondents concentrated on dissemination rather than utilization: "I sent the NORC report with comments on to the assistant secretary's office, but I do not know what happened to it after that."

Second, in some cases, it was possible to assemble detailed histories of the information flows and patterns of utilization. In the energy areas, for example, respondents cited specific use in one policy area and then stated that all or most other cases followed the same pattern. One respondent said, "The weekly reports were received here in the Office of _____ , and we would talk about the results with NORC staff members, and then write a summary of the highlights to be sent to our superiors [the assistant secretary's office]. This summary memo was attached to the actual tabulations submitted by NORC. [See Appendix D for an example.] Our boss then initialed the memo and sent it on to the secretary. I think he took it with him to the Joint-Energy Task Force meetings. As a whole, this same pattern was followed for all the weekly reports." Another detailed history was very similar: "We asked for a specific set of information on daylight saving time. When I received the results from NORC, I immediately summarized the results, placed them in the context of other information we had gathered on the same question, and sent it on to the assistant secretary and the secretary. The secretary then asked me to brief him on this matter for purposes of press releases and a congressional presentation. The CNS information was very important for our press releases and the congressional presentation."

Third, some respondents were able to give a limited case history, and then other participants were consulted to fully trace patterns of utilization. For example, one respondent reported: "I worked very closely with NORC representatives in writing a paper I produced on the basis of these results. I sent this paper to my superiors and to other assistant secretaries I thought would be interested in this information. I also sent it to some of the program people within our agency who would be interested in this. After some time, I heard that the assistant secretaries were interested in the results and that the results had caused some controversy among the program people. It might have some influence on the bills these assistant secretaries and program administrators are responsible for; but I just don't know." On the basis of these kinds of responses, aggregate categories were constructed. However, it is important to note that this level of detail was sought before any categories were constructed.

In this analysis, two waves of information utilization, with distinctly different profiles, were discovered. To some extent, they may be equated with short-term and long-term utilization. The first wave seems to occur when information is initially received and for approximately three months thereafter. The three-month period is tentative; in this case study, it appears that this is the maximum time it takes for an agency to digest information and have it flow through the decision-making hierarchy if it is to be used on a short-term basis. The first wave can be characterized by the following profile: When the information is used, the flow of information is upward through the decision-making hierarchy and the utilization of information is primarily instrumental. *Instrumental* refers to a use or impact of information that can be documented: it appears directly in a memo to a high-level policy maker, it is used to draft legislation, it is discussed at a cabinet meeting or a meeting of the secretaries or assistant secretaries, or it is used for a congressional briefing. For those agencies receiving the reports provided by NORC, the first wave of utilization is summarized in Table 3.

Table 3. Use of Information (Multiple Responses Are Possible; by Policy Area; N = 26)

Kind of Use	First Wave	Second Wave
None	11	3
Regulation writing	2	0
General background only	6	6
Conceptual use or methodological planning	1	6
Writing memos to counterparts	11	4
Writing memos to supervisors	16	1
Writing memos for congressional presentations	2	0
Writing memos to subordinates	0	17
Briefing assistant secretary	11	0
Briefing secretary	10	0
Briefing joint meeting (cabinet level)	9	0
Writing papers or journal articles	2	9
Writing new RFPs	0	6
Planned use, conceptual	1	21
Planned use, instrumental	1	13
Speech by upper-level policy maker	2	0

There may be multiple uses within a given policy area. By way of interpretation, it should be noted that in eleven of the policy areas no use was made of the information—the information simply sat on the desk of the staff member who initially received it. This does not mean that the information was not used in the second wave of utilization. The most common uses were memos to supervisors, briefings for the assistant secretary or some large staff meeting, and memos to counterparts. Such uses do not necessarily reflect a direct application to problem solving in the policy area. The least common forms of utilization were the writing of new RFPs, papers for journals or books, regulations, and memos to subordinates in the decision-making hierarchy. These types of utilization are least applicable to policy and the most appropriate for individual career advancement.

In terms of the first wave of utilization, there are also patterns related to the dissemination of information. Memos, letters, or reports were sent to counterparts, supervisors, assistant secretaries, and secretaries in a substantial number of policy areas during this first wave. In eight of the policy areas in which information was not used for any purpose during the first wave, there was an application of the information in the sending of a memo or report to a counterpart; in five of the eleven cases in which the information was not used, a memo or report was sent to a supervisor. The other cases in which information was disseminated did not overlap with the policy areas in which the information was not utilized. Thus, in at least eight of the eleven policy areas in which the information was not used, it did not simply sit on the desk of the staff member who initially received it. These results concerning the dissemination of information reflect the use that was planned for the information not utilized instrumentally during the first wave (see Table 4).

Table 4. Flows of Information (Multiple Responses Are Possible; by Policy Areas; $N = 26$)

Disposition of Information	First Wave	Second Wave	Planned Use
Upward within agency	13	3	5
Upward elsewhere in department	7	3	2
Upward elsewhere in government	4	3	0
Lateral	5	10	9
Downward within agency	2	9	5
Downward elsewhere	6	7	1
Remained on desk	11	3	7

The second wave of utilization generally occurred from three to six months after the information was initially received, though it also may have occurred at a later time. The flow of information in this case is primarily lateral or downward in the decision-making hierarchy (see Table 4) and the utilization of information is primarily conceptual in nature. *Conceptual* refers to uses that influence a policy maker's thinking about an issue without any direct instrumental use. It also refers to uses in the area of methodological planning: influences on the way in which RFPs are written, influences on future selection of methodological instruments and analytic procedures. Social science information has been traditionally used by federal policy makers for conceptual purposes: for conferences, for journal papers, for general background only, and for purposes of writing new RFPs.

For the second wave, many found that the CNS had a profound conceptual effect. By far, the most prevalent form of utilization was a memo to subordinates in the decision-making hierarchy concerning general notions and ideas that had been teased out of the CNS results. The other kinds of uses documented during this second wave reflect the nature of such memos. First, there are a significant number of cases in which the respondents' thinking was affected by the results of the survey (general background or conceptual use). Second, a significant number of journal articles and papers were written on the basis of the CNS results. New RFPs were also written or influenced by the survey results. Finally, in the vast majority of cases (thirty-four policy areas) the respondents had concrete plans for utilizing the CNS results in the future. This last finding reflects the profound conceptual effect of the second wave. Policy makers and their staffs continued to think about the results, although they had not yet put them to any direct instrumental use.

The second wave also reflects a pattern different from the first wave in terms of the application of information. There were far fewer instances of applying information in general; they were limited to sending information downward in the decision-making hierarchy. As with the first wave, most of the information that was not utilized was at least disseminated to different parts of the department. During the second wave there were only three policy areas in which the information was not used for conceptual or instrumental purposes (see Table 3).

An analysis of the two waves of utilization should address one other significant issue: Can the different profiles be explained by the argument that the potential for instrumental use was exhausted during the first wave of utilization and, therefore, one could not discover significant levels of instrumental use at a later time? Three points are relevant to this question. In many of the policy areas no use was made of the information during the first wave of utilization; yet, during the interviews respondents reported that they planned to make some instrumental use of this information in the future. For example, one respondent said: "I collected this long-term trend information for the purpose of aiding the planning process and writing legislation in the area of facilitating travel between large cities. We just haven't had the time to get to it yet. I hope that within the next six to nine months this will be possible." Another respondent articulated the same concern: "Our staff have been told to work with other problems which have been assigned high priority. However, this information will be crucial in drafting legislation and regulations in this area."

In a few cases it is undoubtedly true that a decision was made not to make any instrumental use of the CNS information for high-level policy making. One policy maker, at the assistant secretarial level, made such a decision: "I did not use this information or send it upstairs because I don't see its relevance for the kinds of problems we have to solve. Some of our lower-level staff have expressed interest in this kind of information. If they can use it as part of their general research program, this is fine." This kind of attitude was expressed by only two of the upper-level respondents. In these cases, instrumental use was not exhausted during the first wave, but officials decided not to make instrumental use of the CNS information for high-level policy making at any point in time. In cases in which instrumental use was made of the information during the first wave, it is not possible to judge definitively whether the potential for instrumental utilization was exhausted during the first wave. If one were to limit the analysis of utilization to the correlation between expected and actual use one could reach a definitive judgment on this issue. However, as we have already discovered, utilization cannot be delimited by that correlation.

Our analysis thus far shows that short-term information, related to a "hot issue," is more valued by upper-level policy makers than any other kind of information. The correlation between expected and actual use was significantly higher for the "hot issues" than for other kinds of questions asked through the CNS instrument. It is undoubtedly true that in the short run the potential for instrumental use may have been exhausted, within the limits of the correlation between expected and actual utilization. However, we must also remember that the information may prove to be important for writing future legislation and decisions concerning utilization may be reversed.

The policy-making agenda changes daily; information is collected to meet the immediate short-term needs and is stored for possible use in addressing new problems as they arise. As a result, the potential for instrumental use may be great; this is built into the procurement process. Thus, one cannot conclude that the profiles are different because the potential for instrumental use was exhausted during the first wave. The expected uses were met in a limited number of cases; in this specific sense, the potential for use was exhausted. However, this finding does not imply that the overall potential for instrumental use was exhausted. There are other important factors which contribute to the characteristics of these profiles.

These two waves of utilization reflect what might be called very high levels of utilization. Since the universe of information available for potential use is unknown, it is not possible to make absolute statements concerning levels of utilization. Relative to what the literature would have one believe, these results reflect amazingly high levels of utilization. Relative to expectations on the basis of knowledge of how the information was collected, the levels of utilization were low; that is, the correlation between expected and actual uses was low. However, we gleaned a very different picture from the analysis of the two waves of utilization. It seems less important to make a determination concerning quantity than to compare use and nonuse and to illustrate diverse kinds of utilization.

Differences Between Kinds of Questions. The analyses of these data point to important differences between the uses made of questions related to program areas and those related to policy areas. The program questions were primarily put to conceptual use and the policy questions were primarily put to instrumental use (see Table 5). We divide the uses between instru-

Table 5. Uses by General Policy Areas
(Multiple Responses Are Possible; N = 26)

Kind of Use	Program Areas	Policy Areas
Instrumental	6	11
Conceptual	12	6
No use	2	1

mental and conceptual because of a "cell problem." Since there are a limited number of policy areas to be divided over three kinds of questions, if each kind of instrumental and conceptual use for each of the three kinds of questions were included, there would not be enough cases in any one cell for purposes of analysis. The differentiation among hot issues, monitoring, and methodological questions does less well in explaining differences between instrumental and conceptual use than the distinction between program and policy. However, two points can be made by way of interpretation: the "hot issue" questions are not used conceptually, and the "hot issue" items were all put to some use (see Table 6). The results do not allow comparative

Table 6. Uses by Type of Question (Multiple Responses Are Possible;
by Policy Area; N = 26)

Kind of Use	Hot Issue	Methodological	Monitoring
Instrumental	8	0	8
Conceptual	2	2	9
No use	0	0	3

statements concerning the three types of questions. Similarly we find that attitudinal questions were primarily used conceptually; but, we cannot make significant distinctions between the social inventory and evaluative questions.

Differences Between Energy and Nonenergy Policy Areas. Related to the question of differences between kinds of questions is the analysis of differences between policy areas. As illustrated in Table 7, the most important difference in this study is

Table 7. Kinds of Use in Energy and Nonenergy Policy Areas
(Multiple Responses Are Possible; $N = 26$)

Kind of Use	Energy		Nonenergy	
	First Wave	Second Wave	First Wave	Second Wave
No use	2	1	9	2
General background	3	1	3	5
Conceptual	0	0	1	6
Regulation writing	1	0	1	0
Memos to counterparts	9	1	2	3
Memos to supervisors	10	0	6	0
Memos for congressional presentations	2	0	1	0
Joint meeting at cabinet level	9	0	0	0
Writing papers or journal articles	0	4	2	5
Writing RFPs	0	2	0	4
Planned use, conceptual	1	10	0	11
Planned use, instrumental	1	10	0	3
Speeches	0	0	2	0
Briefing assistant secretary	8	0	2	0
Briefing secretary	8	0	3	2
Sent to Congress	2	0	0	4
Sent to counterpart	9	0	2	1
Sent to supervisor	9	0	2	0
Sent to subordinate	0	9	0	2
Sent to assistant secretary	9	0	2	1
Sent to secretary	9	0	2	0
Sent to others	—	—	—	3

the one between the energy-related and nonenergy-related areas. The information collected concerning the energy crisis in general and the impact of the Arab oil embargo in specific was used more consistently for instrumental purposes than the information collected in any other policy area. It is also in these areas that the information was put to the most diverse use and applications. In the energy areas, the differences between the first and second waves of utilization were still maintained. Relative to the energy areas, however, the other policy areas reflect very limited instrumental use and greater conceptual use in the second wave.

The greatest discrepancy between the two policy areas is illustrated by the category "joint meetings at the cabinet level." In the energy areas this is one of the most significant kinds of instrumental use; in the other areas it is one of the least significant. The number of instances of use for the purpose of joint meetings reflects the coordination between the participating agencies and the formulation of questions for this policy area. However, this cooperation did not ensure that the agencies would use the information in the same way. Typically, the secretaries attending these joint meetings brought the NORC reports and staff memos related to these reports with them. Within the agencies there were discrepancies in utilization in two of the six energy areas. These differences are far less important than the fact that three secretaries brought information from the CNS data to the same policy meeting.

Policy Makers' Involvement in Questionnaire Formulation. Our analysis of utilization also includes a review of differences in utilization related to administrative and structural factors that developed during the CNS project. The extent to which policy makers were involved in the formulation of questions appears to have some effect on utilization. For this particular analysis, distinctions between direct involvement, indirect involvement, and no involvement were made. These categories were derived from interviews and the analysis completed in Chapter Four. In terms of utilization, a distinction was made between instrumental, conceptual, and no utilization. When policy makers were directly involved, utilization was primarily instrumental in nature; and when involvement was indirect, use seemed to be more conceptual (see Table 8).

In examining utilization, we wanted to determine whether there were significant differences between upper-level policy makers and other staff in the kinds of use they made of the in-

Table 8. Use by Extent of Involvement by Policy Makers in Question Formulation (Multiple Responses Are Possible; by Policy Area; N = 26)

	Involvement		
Kind of Use	Direct	Indirect	None
Instrumental	10	5	0
Conceptual	2	17	1
None	4	4	1

formation. As one would expect, Table 9 shows that upper-level policy makers put the information more consistently to instrumental use than other staff members did. This difference re-

Table 9. Comparison of Upper-Level Policy Makers and Other Staff (by Respondents; N = 35)

Kind of Use	Upper-Level Policy Makers	Other Staff
Instrumental	9	8
Conceptual	11	16
None	2	3

flects the fact that by the time information reaches a policy maker, some determinations have already been made with respect to the appropriate use of the information. In this context, we should also note that the differences between upper-level policy makers and others in terms of use are not as great as one might have expected. The literature leads one to expect that lower-level policy makers use information conceptually and pass it upward through the decision-making hierarchy for the purposes of instrumental use. Our findings show that there is diversity in kinds of utilization at all levels in the decision-making hierarchy.

Agencies that Continued to Fund the CNS Compared with Those that Did Not. We can also analyze the extent to which administrative decisions concerning the CNS affected the levels of utilization by comparing those agencies that committed funds to NORC and those that did not. Because of the

cell problems already discussed, distinctions were made only between agencies in which NORC diversified and those in which it
did not. In terms of utilization, three categories were viewed:
instrumental, conceptual, and no use.

Whether an agency continued to fund the CNS appears to
be independent of the use it made of the results received from
NORC. However, as with policy makers' involvement in questionnaire formulation, NORC's success in diversifying did seem
to affect utilization. Where the project was diversified there was
significantly more instrumental use than where it was not. However, this category, too, does not predict well for nonutilization. Furthermore, nondiversification does not distinguish as
well between instrumental and conceptual use as diversification
does.

Trusted Staff Aides. Given the nature of the information
collected and the administrative problems associated with this
project, it is necessary to concentrate on differences in utilization related to the transmission of information. The literature
suggests that the status of the individual or group passing information to a policy maker is critical to utilization. Empirical
studies have shown that policy makers distrust the motives of
those passing information to them. Do they seek to gain status
for themselves? Do they understand the policy problems facing
the decision maker? Do they subordinate their personal goals in
relation to career advancement to the success of the problem-
solving process? Researchers within the government and within
the academic community tend not to be trusted because they
do not understand policy problems. They seek to optimize personal career advancement, and their motivations for passing on
information are questionable. The history of CNS also indicates
that trust is important.

Thus, if policy makers cannot rely on their own knowledge and expertise, they go to the staff aide from whom they
got reliable (trustworthy) information the last time a problem
arose in the policy area now under consideration. The more
times a policy maker has found an individual to be reliable, the
greater is the individual's chance to gain access to the secretary
or other upper-level policy makers. The combination of unques-

tionable motivations and goals and accessibility to the policy maker distinguishes trusted staff aides from other staff aides.

Our study shows that information passed on by a trusted staff aide is utilized far more often for instrumental purposes than information transmitted by other staff members. Policy makers and their staffs were relied upon to indicate who the trusted staff aides were. Furthermore, this category also distinguishes well for nonutilization: When information is passed on by a trusted aide, it will be utilized, and when it is not, it may not be. This factor distinguishes more clearly between the three categories of utilization than any of the factors discussed earlier.

Research Skills of the Agency Participants. Given the importance of trust in effecting utilization, it is also interesting to discover whether differences in a participant's training and familiarity with research skills influenced levels of utilization. Respondents were divided into two categories: those with some training in research methodology and those with little or no training. The majority of respondents had some training in research methodology. For those with research training, little significant differentiation between instrumental and conceptual utilization was found. Respondents were also divided into the category of users and nonusers. Our results reveal little differentiation between users and nonusers relative to their background in research methodology. However, the interviews do suggest that those with greater familiarity with survey research and more intensive training in research methodology were the ones who first perceived the usefulness of CNS. They also were the ones best able to clearly define the questions they were interested in asking and their policy applications and uses. These results would, therefore, suggest that as the respondents with less training gained experience with CNS, initial differentiations relative to receptivity and use would become indistinguishable. At this point, it is worth noting that individual differences in background are to be distinguished from organizational differences in rank and department. They are also to be distinguished from differences relative to the confidence a particular upper-level policy maker has in a staff member. Background and training of the individual participants are not as important as a direct link to a policy maker.

Analysis of Patterns of Utilization

In general this study shows that administrative, organizational, and structural (relative to the decision-making hierarchy) factors better distinguish between utilization and nonutilization, on the one hand, and instrumental and conceptual utilization, on the other, than differences in individual qualifications. This finding is consistent with those cited in Chapter Five.

Respondents were asked to identify the factors that are critical to an understanding of why information is utilized by policy makers. Each active agency participant was given ten factors that might be important in the understanding of utilization and was asked to identify each as of great importance, some importance, or little importance.

Each of the factors mentioned to the respondents represents an exact quotation from the literature on utilization concerning the most important factors that determine utilization or (much less frequently) a factor mentioned by some respondents during earlier interviews. As Table 10 shows, six factors were identified as of great importance in the understanding of utilization:

1. The information supports the policy position that the decision maker is predisposed toward.
2. The information comes directly to the decision maker from a trusted staff aide.
3. The information is on a timely topic that is of interest and need.
4. The objectivity of the producer is unquestionable.
5. The information is written up in a manner that is understandable.
6. The information does not challenge the budget or staff allocations of the agency.

The two factors mentioned as least important by the re-

Table 10. Factors Affecting Utilization (Multiple Responses Are Possible; by Respondent; N = 18)

Factor	Great Importance	Some Importance	Little Importance
Information supports a pre-disposed policy position	10	7	1
It comes directly to a decision maker through a trusted staff aide	13	5	0
It has not moved up through the hierarchy, but came in laterally	0	7	11
It is generated in-house	0	12	6
It is on a timely topic of interest	15	2	1
It is a unique source of information	0	2	16
The objectivity of the producer is unquestionable	13	5	0
It is written up in an understandable manner	4	2	2
It does not challenge a position already taken by a policy maker	1	10	7
It does not challenge the budget or staff allocations of the agency	10	3	5

spondents were "it is a unique source of information," and "the information does not challenge a position already taken by a policy maker." In explaining the low priority given to these two factors, respondents contended that a unique source of information would be of little value because it could not be collaborated or validated by other sources. Multiple studies are commissioned or contracted on the same topic in order to provide validation. Thus, it is natural to find that validation is valued in the process of utilization. In addition, respondents said that a policy maker cannot afford to ignore information that challenges a policy position already taken. The decision maker could potentially harm himself and his position by ignoring information rather than seeking to come to terms with it. Respondents differentiated between this factor and the one concerning the collection of information to support a policy position, which they consider to be quite important. Collecting information to serve one's purposes was clearly distinguished in the minds of our respondents from ignoring information already collected.

In this same context, respondents were asked to identify which of these factors were the most important for understanding utilization. The majority of the respondents were careful to point out that the objectivity of the producer and the timeliness of the topic must be assumed. Otherwise, the information would either not be collected or not be sent through the decision-making hierarchy for possible use. Thus, the question of which factor is most important in understanding utilization must be approached with the assumption that the other two conditions have first been met. That the information "comes directly to the decision maker through a trusted staff aide" is identified as the one most important factor in the understanding of utilization. This finding is consistent with one cited earlier: Whether the information was transmitted by a trusted staff aide made a significant difference relative to distinguishing between conceptual and instrumental use as well as utilization and non-utilization.

These results provide evidence for the argument that information is used or not used depending on whether its use would violate organizational interests within the limited context of purely administrative factors. One indicator of organizational interest (bureaucratization) is: "Only information provided by a proven source is utilized." Policy makers consciously try to minimize risk in relation to their own position and the position of their organization. They cannot afford to be embarrassed by the results of a study or other information that has been submitted to a superior. They, therefore, seek to rely upon an aide who understands their position and who will measure considerations of risk before the information is submitted. This notion of risk also implies that trade-offs are consciously made in policy decisions, as was well illustrated in the analysis of funding decisions in Chapter Five.

Another indicator of this same phenomenon is the extent to which information is used or not used relative to the extent to which it challenges an agency's budget or staff allocations. Although this factor was not cited as one of the most important by the respondents, it was identified as having great importance. These results offer additional evidence for the argument concerning organizational interests in that the extent to which information supports a policy position that a decision maker is predisposed toward is also identified as a very important factor in understanding utilization. However, this preliminary analysis of the extent to which organizational interests are manifested in decisions concerning the utilization of information is not exhaustive nor is it meant to suggest that absolute support for the bureaucratization hypothesis has been provided.

The second most important factor for the understanding of utilization, identified by respondents, is that the information is written in a manner that is understandable. This factor is an indicator for the communications gap that supposedly exists between researchers and policy makers. The form in which information is passed through the decision-making channels is often of greater importance than its content. *Form* refers to the length of a memo, its precision in defining terms, and its ability to relate data to the policy agenda and problem conceptualization of the policy maker. In interviews respondents constantly reported a concern over differences in time perceptions between policy makers and researchers. Policy makers want a short, concise memo whose relevance to the problem under investigation is immediately apparent. Researchers do not express the same sense of urgency felt by policy makers. They would rather not write a memo if the research upon which it is based is not completed. They perceive preliminary results as invalid; therefore, they resist transmitting them through the decision-making channels.

If a memo cannot be immediately understood because of its form, its content is rejected. Again, the notion of risk is of some importance in the analysis of this factor. If a policy maker cannot understand a memo, it is not in his interests to use it. By itself, this conclusion does not represent evidence in support of the organizational interest argument. It is conceivable to argue that anyone, in or out of an organization, would reject a memo for use if it was not understandable. However, it also seems natural to assume that if the information could be of potential importance in relation to a problem to be solved, one would seek further explanation or a redraft of a memo before rejecting its content. On the basis of the interviews conducted for this study, it was not possible to conclude that problem solving was taking place in this manner.

This finding concerning form is consistent with the one concerning trusted staff aides. To some extent, policy makers rely on trusted staff aides because they have not experienced satisfactory performance by other staff members. Form is particularly important when it is considered in conjunction with who is transmitting the information. Trusted aides tend to institutionalize a preference for certain types of form over others.

In terms of the different policy areas to which the CNS was applied, the most salient distinction documented was between energy and nonenergy areas. In the energy areas, the CNS results were put more consistently to instrumental use than in any of the other policy areas. The factors related to the use of the energy data are somewhat different than those influencing the other policy areas. Factors such as the quality and form of the information were generally of greater or equal importance to the organizational ones. In the energy areas, the single most important factor in understanding utilization is whether the information was transmitted by a trusted staff aide. However, the importance assigned to this factor compared to the factors relating to the quality of information is by no means as great as it is in the other policy areas.

The diminished importance of the organizational factors in the energy areas seems related to the differences in the factors concerning the procurement of this information—people were willing to share information because of the crisis. The use of the energy data appears to be influenced by a set of conditions that did not affect the other policy areas:

1. There was little, if any, available in-house data.
2. There were few energy experts in the federal bureaucracy; energy had not been studied systematically by federal policy makers.
3. Institutionalized channels of decision making were not established in this policy area when the crisis arose.
4. There was a willingness among departments and agencies to cooperate in finding solutions.
5. High-level policy makers were willing and eager to read as much as possible in this policy area to establish a reservoir of expertise.

These conditions would seem to explain why the information flowed consistently to the top of the decision-making hierarchy and why there was such a willingness to undertake multiagency cooperation and problem solving. The opposite of these conditions would seem to explain the patterns of utilization for the more established or traditional federal bureaucracies.

Participants' responses to the question about factors critical to the understanding of utilization also provide some evidence for the argument. Participants concentrated more on factors relating to the quality of information in this policy area because of the importance of information resources in developing organizational expertise in each of the participating departments. The hypothesis could be extended that as expertise develops in the energy areas and as organizational decision-making channels become more institutionalized, these policy areas will begin to resemble the others. This analysis suggests that organizational factors affect policy areas in a differential manner. These results may also suggest a general distinction between responses to a crisis and other responses.

The factors cited by upper-level policy makers were compared to the ones cited by those in lower-level positions. No significant differences emerge from this analysis. Researchers tend to be more concerned with the properties of information that relate to quality, and policy makers are more concerned with organizational factors. This is consistent with our other findings.

In relation to factors that are critical to the understanding of utilization, a general distinction between users and non-users of the CNS information was made. Users includes those participants who made some use of the information, and non-users includes those who made absolutely no use of the information. There are no significant differences between the users and nonusers in the factors they identified as critical to the understanding of utilization. However, there were some differences in the factors identified as most important for the understanding of utilization. Nonusers tended to emphasize the form in which the information was transmitted more than the users. Users emphasized organizational factors relating to collecting information to support a policy position and processing information in terms of whether it challenged a budget or staff allocation. These differences are, however, only suggestive.

This last set of results would seem to point to the importance of the communications gap between researchers and policy makers highlighted in the literature. The results concerning utilization and concerning the extent to which use expectations were realized also support this argument. However, the communications-gap theory implicitly argues that information generated by researchers is not used by policy makers. Even though a strong correlation was not documented between expected and actual use, much of the information was utilized, instrumentally or conceptually, six months subsequent to receipt of the information. This combination of results suggests that some intervening variable is operating. Organizational and administrative factors seem to explain these results. Policy makers are receptive to survey research information and use it instrumentally and conceptually for policy and program purposes. The fact that a piece of information is not utilized for the purpose expected does not substantiate the argument that a communications gap is the most important factor in an understanding of utilization. It does, however, suggest that in the transmission of information there is one critical factor or condition that helps to determine whether information will be used. This study points to policy makers' reliance on a proven source of information: the trusted staff aide. This aide makes qualitative judgments concerning information; however, these judgments do not gain him continuous access to the policy maker. Instead, the organizational judgments concerning risks and trade-offs relative to the use of the information are the determinants of access.

Respondents were also asked to compare the use they made of the information provided by CNS to other social science information available to them, to information provided through the press or popular journals, and to information generated in-house. In-house information was used more consistently than any of the other sources available to the policy makers in the areas in which CNS data was requested (see Table 11). In-house sources are, of course, the sources that bureaucrats are accustomed to and have had long-term experience with. As a result, they are able to assess the strengths

Table 11. Use of CNS Information Compared to Other Available Information (Greater, Less, or Equal Use Compared to CNS; by Policy Area; N = 26)

Agency	Press	Other Social Science Information	In-House Information
1	Less than, except one area	More than, except energy	Greater than, all areas
2	Greater than, except energy	Greater than, except energy	Greater than, except energy
3	Greater than, all areas	Greater than, all areas	Greater than, all areas
4	Less than, all areas	Less than, all areas	Equal use, all areas
5	Greater than, all areas	Equal use, all areas	Greater than, all areas
6	Less than, all areas	Equal use, all areas	Greater than, all areas
7	Less than, all areas	Greater than, all areas	Greater than, all areas
8	Less than, all areas	Equal use, all areas	Equal use, all areas
9	Greater than, all areas	Greater than, all areas	Greater than, all areas

and weaknesses related to these data. The policy maker can also feel more comfortable in using in-house sources because risks can be fully judged. Other social science information and the press also tended to be used more than the CNS data. The respondents explained that this latter judgment was more difficult to make. However, in the energy areas the CNS information was used more consistently than the other two kinds. This finding is consistent with the general differences between energy and nonenergy areas. Moreover, respondents explained that the factors affecting the use of the CNS information were not different from those affecting the use of the other two sources. On the contrary, the organizational factors already outlined help to explain why in-house information was given more attention than other kinds.

Finally, in relation to general utilization, the interviews reveal that the predominant assumptions of federal policy makers with respect to social science information (that it is difficult to apply to short-term policy needs, difficult to understand, and not timely) were confirmed by their experience with CNS. Even though levels of utilization appear to be relatively high, policy makers' attitudes toward the producers of this kind of information did not change significantly. Once an agency has committed budget or staff resources to a source of information, it is committed to making some use, somewhere within the department, of it. For policy makers who must justify a budget and allocations of other staff resources, it is not feasible to write off a project for which resources were committed. If they did, it would reflect badly on their management skills and on the efficiency of departmental operations.

This analysis is limited by its focus on utilization. As with other studies, these results only indicate whether a piece of information was used, in some way, at some time during the life of the project. They do not indicate what portions of the original NORC reports were used, the form in which the information was passed through the decision-making channels, and the criteria used for selecting information to be sent through the decision-making channels. This analysis also does not reveal who received the information nor the places in the decision-making hierarchy to which it was sent. These latter concerns reflect the dissemination of information resources.

Flow and Application of CNS Information

The transmission of information occurred in clusters centered around all the issues applying in a particular policy area. In the energy policy areas, more frequent reports were transmitted to policy makers concerning the same set of questions. In some cases there were weekly reports, and in other policy areas there were two or three memos, letters, or reports focusing on the same policy area. In the nonenergy policy areas, staff members waited until all the information was received from NORC before transmitting it through the decision-making channels.

With the exception of two cases, NORC contacts within the agencies' decision-making hierarchy were two steps below the level of assistant secretary. If information was to reach the assistant secretary's desk, it had to go through the contact's boss and then be sent to the assistant secretary. The assistant secretary could then send information directly to the secretary. In the other two cases, NORC was in direct communication with a special assistant who reported to a secretary and an assistant secretary. These special assistants were in the position to write memos directly to the secretary or assistant secretary. Thus, the flow of information upward through the decision-making hierarchy followed one of six basic patterns:

1. The information came to the staff member in contact with NORC and he did not send it to anyone.
2. The staff member received a NORC report and sent it on to his boss, who did not send it any further.
3. The staff member sent the information to his boss, who passed it on to an assistant secretary, who did not pass it on.
4. The assistant secretary received the information and sent it on to the secretary.
5. A special assistant received the information and passed it on directly to the secretary.

6. A special assistant received the information and decided not to pass it on.

Information that does not flow upward in the decision-making hierarchy may be passed on to colleagues at the same level or passed downward. The direction of information's movement in the decision-making hierarchy may change at any point, or it may flow out of the agency to a different branch of government, for example, the Congress. An assistant secretary could, for example, receive a report and decide that it should be sent downward in the decision-making hierarchy, below the point at which it entered. Furthermore, information may be transmitted in two different directions at the same time (for example, lateral and upward).

In each of the interviews, respondents were asked to specify where in the decision-making hierarchy the CNS information was sent. On the basis of these interviews, diagrams were constructed illustrating the flow of information.

Earlier we concluded that the basic flow of information was upward during the first wave of utilization and lateral or downward during the second wave. In the vast majority of policy areas, the CNS information was applied in one of four ways:

1. It sat on the desk of the staff member receiving it during the first wave and was transmitted laterally and downward during the second wave.
2. It flowed laterally and upward during the first wave and downward during the second wave.
3. The information flowed exclusively upward during the first wave and laterally during the second wave.
4. The information flowed upward during the first wave and remained at that level during the second wave.

Usually, information sent upward was also made available to colleagues within the same office. Although one could count these instances as information moving in two directions at the same time, it is more accurate to conclude that the information was flowing primarily in one direction.

The flows of information were not difficult to trace (see Table 12). The staff member who initially received the report had three choices: to send the information directly upward through the decision-making hierarchy, to let it remain on his desk until it seemed appropriate to send it upward, or to let it remain on his desk indefinitely. Information was not sent downward, to another department or branch of government, made part of an agency's data bank, used exclusively for the purposes of writing new RFPs, or used for a paper to a professional journal until a decision was made by a supervisor or upper-level policy maker concerning the usefulness of the information. Lower-level staff members waited for their superiors to either use the information or decide that it would not be used instrumentally before disseminating it in some other manner. After the initial decision concerning utilization had been made, staff members wanted to put the information to some use in order to justify its procurement. Failure to apply the information in some manner might reflect badly on future requests for information resources. Therefore, it was in the interests of their particular organizational subunit and their own survival to find someone who might use each information resource. This fact would seem to account for the difficulty some analysts have found in tracing information flows. By following the flows over time one can point to the decisions and options available to the individuals responsible for transmitting information.

An analysis of the dissemination of information is, of course, not an analysis of utilization. By tracing the transmission of information, we are able to identify potential uses that might be made of particular information. Thus, an analysis of dissemination represents the first step in the analysis of utilization: assessing all the potential uses for a particular information resource.

The patterns we traced of the flow of information within user agencies show that the CNS data were generally not communicated directly to those near or at the top of the organizational hierarchy. Instead, as illustrated by Figure 3, information entered the decision-making system at the bottom. Of the thirty-five reports produced by NORC, information from six

Table 12. Information Flows; Step by Step (Multiple Responses Are Possible; by Policy Area; $N = 26$)

Policy Area	Step 1	Step 2	Step 3	Step 4
		Agency 1		
Monitoring	Sent to boss	Sent to assistant secretary	Sent downward	
Evaluative	Sat on desk—not sent yet			
Monitoring	Sent to boss	Sent to assistant secretary and presented in professional paper	Sent downward, and sent elsewhere in government	
Evaluative	Sent to boss and laterally	Sent to assistant secretary	Used for professional paper	
		Agency 2		
Evaluative	Sent to boss	Sent to assistant secretary and laterally to colleagues	Sent to Congress	
Evaluative	Not sent yet (planned)	To assistant secretary		
Monitoring	Not sent yet (planned)	To assistant secretary		
		Agency 3		
Evaluative	Just sat			
Monitoring	Just sat			
Monitoring	Sent to colleagues; released to the public; sent to boss	Boss sent laterally	Sent to institute director	
		Agency 4		
Monitoring	Sat on desk	Sent downward		
Evaluative	Sat on desk			

Monitoring	Sent to boss	Sent downward		
Monitoring areas together	Sent to boss	Sent to assistant secretary and secretary	Used in cabinet meeting	
Evaluative and monitoring	Sent to assistant secretary	Sent to secretary	Used in cabinet meeting	Congressional presentation
Attitudinal	Sent to boss	Sent to assistant secretary		
Agency 5				
Evaluative	Just sat			
Evaluative	Just sat			
Monitoring	Sent to boss and laterally	Sent to assistant secretary	Sent to secretary	To cabinet meeting
Monitoring	Sent to boss	Sent to assistant secretary and downward	Secretary	
Evaluative	Sent to boss and laterally	Sent to secretary	Released to public	
Agency 6				
Monitoring together	Sent to boss and laterally	Sent to assistant secretary	Sent to secretary	To cabinet-level meeting
Attitudinal	Sent to boss	Sent to assistant secretary	Sent downward	Sent elsewhere in government
Evaluative	Just sat			
Evaluative and monitoring	Sent to boss	Sent to assistant secretary	Sent to secretary	
Agency 7				
Monitoring	Sent to boss	Sent downward	Released to public	

Figure 3. Summary of Information Flow for Thirty-Five Requested
Research Inputs

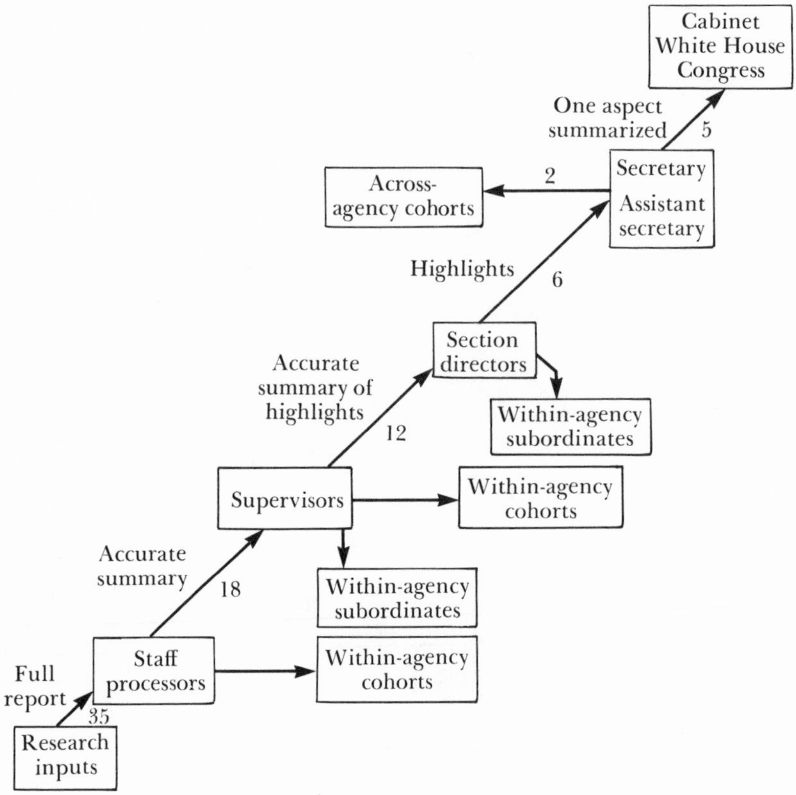

(17 percent) of the CNS reports reached upper-level policy makers (secretary or assistant secretary). Information from five of these six reached the cabinet, the White House, or Congress.

As the information travels upward, not only is the number of reports from which information is drawn progressively reduced but the amount of information transmitted from these remaining reports is also drastically reduced. Staff processors who initially receive the information usually acquire the full report. Information from only about one half of the reports is passed on from those who initially receive the data. The information is summarized before it is communicated to their supervisors at the next level in the organizational hierarchy.

This condensation process, however, makes it essential that the persons at the top of the hierarchy trust those who provide them with information and that they have confidence that the information transmitted to them can be substantiated. Thus, it is no surprise that the majority of respondents reported that the most important factor affecting utilization was that the information came to the policy maker through a trusted aide. Other data in this study verify that trust supersedes timeliness, objectivity, political feasibility, and other such variables more typically thought to affect utilization. Of fifteen CNS reports transmitted to policy makers by staff members they identified as trusted aides, all were read and the information from eleven was used in decision making. By contrast, of seventeen reports transmitted to policy makers by other staff persons, five were not read, eight were read but not used, and only four were actually applied to a policy issue.

These results reflect the findings of other studies that characterize bureaucratic policy-making agencies by very strict and differentiated decision-making hierarchies. Staff members gain their rewards and punishments from their boss and his superiors, not from other members of the same department or other agencies. These other colleagues have their own decision-making channels to which they are responsible. Staff members do not get rewarded by their superiors for interesting other agencies, other departments, or other branches of government in using information. Usually those other agencies did not commit budgetary and staff resources to developing the information. Furthermore, individuals' prestige and the prestige of their agency will be enhanced only if the usefulness of the information is recognized by their superiors. Thus, the more complicated information flows seem to reflect the fact that initial applications of information were not realized and thus the information is transmitted in other directions in order to justify its having been collected.

However, as with the discussion of utilization, these results do not indicate anything about selective applications of information. We will now examine the form in which information was transmitted and used and the criteria for selection.

Selectivity

For the eleven policy areas in which information was not sent on during the first wave of utilization, respondents were asked to report in detail why they chose not to pass the CNS information upward through the decision-making hierarchy. Usually, the respondents felt that they had to choose between the results of the CNS study and other kinds of information available to them. Their responses to these questions are summarized in Table 13. We see that "relying upon a proven source

Table 13. Decisions Not to Transmit CNS Information

Reason	Number of Areas
Concern over control of information	1
Confirms judgment of policy maker	4
Actively looking for information to back up predisposed position	3
Relying upon proven source	7
Concern over quality of information	2
Information irrelevant to present policy	1
Timeliness, other reasons	4

of information (not the CNS)" was the factor most consistently cited in influencing decisions not to transmit the CNS information.

One respondent said: "To speak quite frankly, I did not bother to send the NORC information all the way upstairs. It is not that they [upper-level policy makers] are not interested in survey research results. But, one of NORC's competitors has cornered the market. They were hired sometime ago, upstairs is happy with them, and they will continue to be relied upon in the future. There was just no way for NORC to break into this market." Whether the information confirmed the predisposed position of a policy maker was a factor which was also considered to be important. During an interview, a respondent reported: "I always look for information that speaks to the policy position our boss wants to push for. We are told to do this." Timeliness was another important factor: "Whether or not the information is here when we need it is more important to us than one tenth of a point of precision on a significance scale. If it is late and accurate, we may not be able to use it any more. I would rather rely upon a slightly less accurate source that I know would be delivered on time." A concern over the quality or objectivity of the information was cited by only two respondents as important in influencing their decisions.

These results are very difficult to interpret because of the subjective judgments necessary to coding this item. However, other results already cited in this study collaborate the trends suggested by the last set of results. The influence of a proven source (trusted staff aide) has already been highlighted and its importance relative to understanding the impact of organizational interests on behavior has been illustrated. Therefore, it is not surprising to find this factor the one mentioned most consistently as influencing selectivity. The fact that objectivity is assumed helps in understanding why the quality of information did not play a greater role in decisions of whether to transmit information. Finally, a concern over timeliness speaks to the time pressures felt by decision makers. We have already noted that researchers and policy makers have distinctly different conceptions of time. Policy makers prefer to have limited information while they can use it rather than a completed study after the deadline has already passed for a decision. Although this concern is not directly related to supporting organizational interests, it is clear that there is an indirect connection. Constrained by time, policy makers must rely upon a staff member who is able to provide the needed information within the limits of a tight schedule. In order to minimize risks, policy makers will naturally choose to rely upon individuals with whom they have had experience rather than those with untested potential. The link between organizational interests and timeliness is made through the trusted staff aide. Within the context of a single case study, these data are only suggestive. Factors related to protecting organizational interests do make a difference in this case study.

Given the tentative nature of this item, we examined another way of looking at decisions to transmit information on to decision makers. For fifteen policy areas in which information was transmitted, respondents were asked to explain why the information had been sent. We compared their reasons for deciding to send on information with their reasons for deciding not to send on information; most of the latter, we have already seen, reflected organizational interests. But in deciding to send on information, staff members relied upon their intuition. Intuition, in this case, refers to their experience in dealing with policy makers, their experience in knowing what interests policy makers, and their experience in knowing what will be most helpful to policy makers. Clearly, in describing intuition, respondents were also referring to their understanding of what is politically feasible and the kinds of information that will earn them the respect of policy makers.

Thus there are some major differences in the reasons for sending on information and those for not (see Table 14). Information tended to be passed on because staff perceived it to be of general interest to policy makers or because they were instructed to pass on all information on a particular subject. The next most important factor was that the information pertained to an area important to the staff member's unit. This last factor adds another dimension to our understanding of the manifestations of organizational interests. A staff member passes on information on a particular subject in order to gain a specific advantage for his organizational subunit or himself; the information is transmitted to maximize this interest.

The profiles for decisions not to send on information look somewhat different. The most important criterion appears to be how much information was previously sent on the subject. The next most important criterion is a judgment concerning whether policy makers will be interested in the information. Neither of these factors concerns the quality, objectivity, or cost of the information. These factors appear to be related to the staff member's desire to control the flow of information, to decide what is appropriate to send on to policy makers and what is, or should be, of interest to them. As the literature suggests,

Table 14. Decisions About Transmitting Information
(Multiple Responses Are Possible; by Policy Area; $N = 26$)

Reasons	Fifteen Areas in Which Information Was Sent on	Eleven Areas in Which Information Was Not Sent on
"I was instructed to send all information"	8	0
"Our policy makers aren't interested in this information"	2	5
"This contradicts information already sent"	1	1
"Enough information was sent in this area already"	2	8
"This is an area we are pushing for; so it is important to send the information"	5	0
"This is of general interest"	7	0
"Information was held back because of questions over objectivity"	0	2
"I relied upon my intuition and experience"	11	11
"We haven't worked it up yet"	0	4

this is the function bureaucrats cherish. They seek to maintain it because it provides them with an autonomous position of power. These data on criteria for decisions concerning the transmission of information confirm our finding that organizational interests are a primary consideration in these decisions. Staff members seek to control policy makers' access to information and continue to build their own base of power. However, a significant portion of the responses do not necessarily relate to behavior aimed at maximizing organizational interests. These latter results represent the direct responses of the agency participants. To a great extent, they point to the same phenomena discovered in the subjective coding of the four manifestations of organizational interests.

Another dimension of the issue of selectivity is the form

in which information passes through the decision-making hierarchy. Memos are the most common form of communication within the bureaucracies studied. Full reports of the results submitted by NORC were transmitted in only two of the policy areas, both energy areas. (These were not the weekly reports.) Thus, the question is whether the information was summarized accurately so as to cover all aspects of the data requested, or if certain aspects were highlighted and others ignored. More importantly, were certain aspects highlighted so as to distort the overall results reported by NORC? In the vast majority of policy areas in which the information was sent, one aspect of the report was highlighted using some quotations from the original NORC report (see Table 15). However, the selectivity did not

Table 15. Selectivity in Transmission of Information
(Multiple Responses Are Possible; by Policy Area; $N = 26$)

Kind of Policy	Full Report Sent	Full Report Summarized Accurately		One Aspect Highlighted		Recommendation	
		With Quotes	Without Quotes	With Quotes	Without Quotes	Sent	Not Sent
Energy	2	1	1	2	3	3	5
Nonenergy	0	1	0	7	5	3	5
Total	2	2	1	9	8	6	10

distort or significantly change the results submitted by NORC. The following memo is typical.

From: Assistant Secretary for Policy, Plans
          and International Affairs

To: The Secretary

          Attached is this week's Household Energy
          Survey Report.

          The continued funding of the survey is again
          in doubt. We understand that _____ does
          not have the financial capability, at this

time, to support a $500,000 commitment to you to take over responsibility for the survey by March 1. We understand further, that a letter from _____ is on its way to you requesting your assistance in an interim solution. If no rapid resolution is forthcoming the fieldwork will cease on March 1.

Page 7   Regional reports of trouble getting gas; hardest hit—New England, Pacific Coast, Southern states.

Page 11   The U.S. government is receiving *more blame* for the current energy shortage.

Page 12   66 percent of the respondents believe *individual consumers can solve* the gasoline shortage by cutting back driving.

Page 18A   Reactions to daylight saving: before and after the change.

Page 21   Since January 24 the percentage of respondents who feel that they are able to use their car as much as they want *has dropped* from 70 percent to 45 percent.

Page 22   Respondents are *significantly less satisfied* with how much they can use their cars.

Page 24   Significantly more respondents feel the energy shortage has made their lives *worse*.

Page 30   A major increase in the percentage of respondents feeling fuel for trucks is first priority.

Page 33   A major *decrease* in the percentage of respondents *against* gas rationing since January 24.

Page 57   Respondents are cutting down on car trips for social, recreational, and shopping trips.

Page 65   Respondents report large increases in the price paid for gasoline since October 1973.

Full NORC reports were only summarized, covering all aspects of the report, in a few cases. Also, in about half of the instances some recommendation was made by a staff member on the basis of the CNS results. The reasons cited by respondents for abstracting one portion of the NORC report were the same as the ones cited for selectivity in general. Respondents did not seem to be interested in changing the overall meaning of the results submitted to them, but they wanted to frame the results in a memo to best serve the needs of their organization.

An analysis of utilization, by itself, does not indicate the form used to transmit information or the extent of selectivity, nor does it reveal why one portion of a NORC report was preferred over another. More than any other factor, organizational interests influenced decisions of what to transmit. Policy makers have genuine concerns over the policy relevance and quality of information; they were more important than was hypothesized.

Conclusions

The most important aspects of this chapter concern the interaction between decisions to collect information and decisions to utilize it. Do decisions made in procuring information affect subsequent use? Do policy makers need to be involved in collecting information if they are to use it? Does the policy relevance of the information collected have to be clearly defined if it is to be used? Given the state of knowledge in this field of research, one would assume that decisions made when procuring information would, to a great extent, determine use. One would also expect that if a bureaucracy is working at optimal efficiency, policy makers do not have to be involved in collecting information in order to use it. Information should flow through the regular decision-making channels, be recognized and trusted by policy makers, and be utilized because of its applicability to a particular problem under consideration.

Our findings suggest that these expectations may not be correct. Decisions made concerning utilization during the procurement process tend not to be binding. Information resources tend not to be used for the same purpose for which they were designed. Thus, one cannot predict actual instances of utilization on the basis of expected use. However, one is safe in predicting that some kind of utilization will occur. The extent to which policy makers are involved in decisions concerning procurement does seem to influence how the information is ultimately used. The direct input of a policy maker seems to ensure some instrumental use of the information received.

The degree to which staff members are able to clearly define the policy relevance of the information collected also affects how it is subsequently used. The difference between programmatic and upper-level policy areas indicates that instrumental use is correlated to the clarity of initial definitions about specific policy applications. The concern for finding policy-relevant uses, however vaguely defined, for the information collected yields to a greater concern to justify the staff and budgetary resources devoted to its procurement after the first step in the process of transmitting the information. In other words, once a policy maker initially receives information and makes a decision about its usefulness, staff begin to transmit the information outside their direct chain of command to justify its existence within the context of organizational and administrative factors. On the basis of these findings, it can be concluded that an analyst is able to predict only general levels of utilization by tracing the decisions related to the procurement of it. Thus, the interaction effects are limited.

Our analysis also points to some needed revisions in the dominant assumptions of the literature. The perceived gap between researchers and policy makers is limited to the attitudes of the groups toward each other. The attitudes themselves do not predict well to levels or kinds of utilization. The utilization patterns discovered in our analysis indicate minimal resistance to survey research or social science information in general. Thus, the gap is strictly limited to a communications barrier that does not influence utilization once information begins to flow through departmental decision-making channels.

This study also provides a better understanding of the manifestations and limits of the bureaucratization of the knowledge-inquiry system in determining how information is used. The findings suggest that organizational interests are dominant in influencing decisions to collect information and decisions to use it. Bureaucrats seek control over information resources and process information so as to maximize what they perceive to be the interests of their organization. However, organizational factors are not the sole influence on these decisions.

Contemporary bureaucrats contract for survey research information, use survey research information, and perceive its importance in helping to solve policy problems. The fact that they use this information selectively so as to maximize their own interests does not diminish the importance of the applications and diverse uses made of the CNS information.

In terms of dissemination and utilization of the data generated through the CNS, it is very difficult to judge whether the experiment was successful. It is clear that the information was used both instrumentally and conceptually—especially in energy policy areas. In terms of dissemination, some reports (three of thirty-five) reached cabinet-level officials and the White House. Whether this represents success or failure is almost impossible to judge.

Moreover, this study did not document any deliberate misuse of information—neither in terms of the accuracy of summaries nor in terms of the motivations cited for using information.

Utilization followed in the cases in which all the experimental conditions were met (energy); cases in which utilization did not follow tended to be programmatic rather than policy areas. Except in the energy area, there was no direct correlation between the success of the knowledge-transfer mechanism and levels of utilization.

These conclusions point to the bureaucratization of the knowledge-inquiry system. We have cited several indicators of protecting organizational interest, and a concern for such interests was evident throughout respondents' descriptions of the utilization process.

CHAPTER 7

Future of
Survey Research
for Meeting
National Needs

When RANN was first created, it committed itself to experimental strategies for increasing the relevance of social science knowledge to the needs of policy makers at all levels of government. It was one of the first agencies in the federal government to conduct true quasi-experiments in the area of administrative experimentation.

The originator of the term *quasi-experimental design,* Donald T. Campbell, is also an advocate of administrative experiments of this type. With respect to finding an appropriate solution, he reminds us: "The political stance should be: this is a serious problem. We propose to initiate policy A on an experimental basis. If after five years there has been no significant improvement, we will shift to policy B. By making explicit that a given situation is only one of several that the administrator . . . could in good conscience advocate, . . . the administrator can afford honest evaluation of outcomes. Negative results . . . do not jeopardize his job for his job is to keep after the program until something is found that works" (1971b, p. 29). In the case of knowledge-transfer mechanisms designed to serve multiple purposes for multiple agencies, it is time to shift to policy B.

The Success of CNS

In constructing the design for the CNS experiment, RANN presumed that utilization of social science knowledge is directly correlated to the characteristics of the information or data: timeliness, relevance, cost, political feasibility, form, style, and the like. This assumption naturally leads one to formulate "treatments" designed to increase the overall quality of these knowledge-specific attributes. (For a discussion of knowledge-specific characteristics, see Caplan and others, 1975.)

There is no doubt that the CNS met, in most instances, these criteria for success. The CNS data were relevant, timely, of uniform high quality, in the proper form (as specified by upper-level policy makers); indeed, these attributes were present to a greater degree than in most information sources available to federal officials. Thus, given the design of the experiment, one would expect the knowledge-transfer mechanism to be successful and utilization to follow. Moreover, the experiment should have led to a substantial bridging of the gap between policy makers and researchers.

However, the knowledge-transfer mechanism was not successful if judged by several of the criteria specified by RANN. RANN expected agencies to fund the project from their own budgets so that the CNS fieldwork would become part of the regular information resources within agencies, and federal bureaucrats at all levels of the decision-making hierarchy would learn to make appropriate use of the survey instrument.

RANN felt that there was a need in the federal government for survey research which was not being fulfilled by other tools available to policy makers. Thus, the CNS project was funded to teach policy makers new ways to use survey research; the CNS data were not simply to be applied to the same areas as previous survey research. The CNS information was to be integrated with objective data already possessed by the agency participants. Various criteria were agreed upon by NORC and the initial agency participants at the outset. From RANN's perspective, the CNS project was an experiment to test whether the conditions agreed upon could be met. For the most part, if one applies these criteria, one cannot conclude that the experiment was a success. Accepting RANN's original assumptions about the project, one would expect the levels of utilization to be very low.

Yet, on the basis of this study, one can conclude that the CNS was a major success in terms of utilization of the information generated, the learning experience of bureaucrats, and the institutionalization of the concept of a continuous survey. The information was used extensively and for diverse purposes by agency participants at all levels of the decision-making hierarchy. In relation to utilization, in specific, two waves of utilization with distinctly different profiles were discovered. Our findings also suggest that decisions concerning utilization are ongoing. Information is collected to meet general short-term needs and to build a data bank that can be used to solve problems as they arise. Thus, it is difficult to delimit the usefulness of particular resources, since some use may eventually be found for them.

Most participants learned a good deal about the strengths and weaknesses of a survey research instrument for the purposes of policy making. Initially, they had some difficulty in deciding how to use this tool. Survey research is not the most appropriate tool for market research questions (for example, Do you watch our television program? Do you like it? How many cars do you own?). If the agencies are primarily interested in questions of this kind, other research tools provide the same information at a significantly lower cost. Any survey instrument will collect some demographic information concerning the household (number of appliances, age of the house), but survey instruments are most appropriately used for monitoring public attitudes and preferences over time. This application of the instrument allows policy makers to assess the impact of various policy options. Similarly, the tool is quite capable of providing methodological inputs for the development of quality-of-life measures. By the time the survey went out of the field, the majority of the respondents recognized such appropriate uses and expressed regret that they had not used the CNS instrument primarily for these purposes. In many cases, the CNS was used to supply information that could have been more appropriately collected by other means. That policy makers learned how the instrument should be used speaks to the success of the project. It is an open question, however, whether they will be able to apply this knowledge in the future.

The CNS project was the first time that most respondents had been exposed to the concept of a continuous survey based on a national probability sample. This particular survey instrument was appropriate only for the most general policy concerns that would allow decision makers to assess public reaction to several possible options. For purposes of program evaluation, it would have been necessary to field a survey aimed at specific target populations, and for purposes of long-term, time-series monitoring, it was not necessary to field weekly, national samples.

On the basis of this success, three of the four original participating agencies committed some of their own funds to continue the CNS fieldwork. Another agency committed funds after the initial funding period was over. These agency funds were used to fund the survey for an additional six months. The survey went out of the field in June 1974, and the participating agencies continued to receive reports through the spring of 1975.

The data show that CNS was discontinued because of problems having to do with *administrative coordination, bureaucratic competition,* and *bureaucratic regulations concerning procurement of information.* With one exception, the decisions to discontinue did not at all involve judgments concerning the technical quality of the information. Instead, the main problems concerned the funding mechanism, control of the information, and coordination. When the coordination problems could not be solved, CNS went out of the field. The problem was not that a multiagency project could not be coordinated in

the federal government (several have been), but that the participating agencies could not agree to do it in this case. Their concern for ownership and control took precedence, a situation
reflecting the importance of bureaucratic regulations more than
any other factor.

The main point of these results is that utilization does
not automatically result from the fulfillment of a set of conditions that are *presumed* to be related to the existence of two
cultures. The results indicate that there is a partial communications gap between researchers and policy makers at all levels of
the decision-making hierarchy. However, the observed effects of
this gap were not those that one would have predicted on the
basis of the literature. Instead, this phenomenon appears to be
somewhat more complicated and difficult to tease out of seemingly contradictory results. On the one hand, a majority of respondents expressed the belief that such a gap existed; on the
other, the patterns of utilization and application that were
documented did not support their belief. Bureaucrats are able
to distinguish between attitudes toward researchers in general
and decisions concerning utilization, once the data have been
submitted to them. As already suggested, the discrepancy appears to be directly related to the complex system of organizational rewards and punishments.

RANN was mistaken in its attempt to link a particular
knowledge-transfer mechanism to specific expectations with respect to levels of utilization. From RANN's perspective, the
CNS inadvertently increased the levels of use and sophistication
with respect to survey research among federal policy makers. It
is only inadvertent if one believes that utilization is *dependent*
upon the successful implementation of a particular knowledge-
transfer mechanism.

The Bureaucratization of the Knowledge-Inquiry System

The main significance of the empirical findings of this
study is a contribution to the development of the theory of
knowledge utilization for public policy information. The results
help to clarify the tension between communications theory, on

the one hand, and public administration and organizational theory, on the other. Our analysis of the CNS experiment shows that *all* of the so-called necessary conditions for utilization can be met, and utilization still will not follow. Instead, levels of utilization seem to be controlled by a preoccupation of public officials with issues of ownership and control of information. (The issue of ownership and control is explicated by Caplan and Rich, 1976.)

It is certainly true that factors such as timeliness, cost, and relevance play important roles in influencing utilization; *these are necessary but not sufficient conditions.* Many scholars and public officials have been concerned with these necessary conditions; thus, efforts have been made to increase trust between researchers and civil servants, to deliver information on time, to ascertain that information is relevant and readable. In some cases, a "knowledge broker" has been employed to facilitate the achievement of the necessary conditions. In the case of CNS, brokers were used, and the knowledge-transfer mechanism was designed to bridge *all* the gaps posited by the two-cultures theory.

The main issue with respect to utilization appears to be the organizational and bureaucratic routines and procedures that govern the processing and utilization of information in the seven agencies examined. Issues of control and ownership are formidable obstacles to overcome if one is concerned with increasing levels of knowledge utilization. If the concept of the bureaucratization of information is accurate, it provides a way to redefine the utilization process so as to facilitate theoretical developments (see Caplan and Rich, 1976, for further details).

This study provides a good deal of evidence, in all phases of the knowledge-inquiry system, for the validity of the bureaucratizing hypothesis. In terms of necessary and sufficient conditions, the bureaucratic organizational factors represent the sufficient conditions. The CNS experiment was not unique; bureaucratization appears to affect the operations of federal information policy in general.

Funding. In the funding process, for example, organizational and administrative factors influenced the outcome more than scientific judgments related to the quality of information. This was true of agencies responsible for granting funds as well as the ones applying for them. NORC was motivated more by the desire to gain continuous institutional support than by the central concept of the CNS and its relationship to the effective operations of federal information policy. NSF and RANN felt compelled to expend their funds and therefore sought out potential grantees. Their motivation also seemed to be related more to organizational development and survival than to scientific judgments concerning information resources that would be useful to federal agencies.

The Conduct of Research. The development of the CNS project was greatly influenced by the importance of bureaucratic procedures and regulations. This influence was not peculiar to the CNS project; rather, it seems typical of the federal bureaucracy. The initial tensions that developed between NORC and the agencies illustrate this fact. The participants would probably not have objected to the initial costs of the project, had the costs been accurately predicted. Similarly, agencies are accustomed to delays in meeting schedules, but they want to be informed of them. Respondents stressed that they did not question NORC's technical capabilities nor the quality of the information. All participants were concerned by the cost overruns and the delays; high value was placed on such factors in their evaluation. The difference between technical or scientific judgments and judgments relating to bureaucratic rules indicates the organizational priority given to the latter factors by policy makers. Staff members are not rewarded merely for presenting research of high technical quality. Policy makers assume the technical quality of information transmitted through the decision-making channels. Staff members are rewarded for information that is judged useful by policy makers. Staff members cannot risk not having the needed information to transmit to policy makers at the appropriate time.

The evaluation of risks also influenced the actions of the brokers, who were critical in introducing NORC into the agencies. Depending on their rank and position, they also played a significant role in helping the CNS diversify throughout the departments. However, it was not in the interests of these individuals to become too closely involved in the project. If they were perceived as advocates of the project by their colleagues, their judgment would no longer be valued on this project and, potentially, on other projects of this kind. Thus, when brokers feared their position might come into question, they withdrew some of their active support for the CNS. Similarly, in resolving the project's coordination problems, upper-level policy makers also made trade-offs in order to minimize risks. It is not in the interest of a department to be seen as the sole supporter of a project. Thus, no one agency was willing to continue to support CNS after other agencies declined to help administer the project.

The Use of Research. These same kinds of organizational factors were cited as the most important for an understanding of utilization by policy makers. Information transmitted by a trusted aide is most likely to be used, and this factor was named the best predictor of utilization by respondents.

Indeed, the most important finding of this study concerns the role of trusted staff aides. This role allows us to define the limits of the applicability of organizational factors to the problems under investigation. An individual or group of individuals is responsible for determining an agency's position and resource allocations with respect to a particular policy area. Thus, the behavioral manifestations of organizational interests depend on the extent to which organizational members act consistently to support the determined organizational position. To support the organizational position, each member must resist challenges to budget allocations, staff resources, and prestige. In making choices, each staff member tries to balance the strengths and weaknesses of a particular action so as to avoid risking the organizational position. In this study, the trusted staff aide is paradigmatic for this phenomenon. He or she has gained prestige through continual access to upper-level policy makers. This access, in turn, enables the aide to claim a large budget and to enjoy the full confidence of the secretary. Trusted staff aides are, therefore, constantly in the position of making trade-offs to maintain their organizational stature. The interviews show that other respondents would like to become like the trusted staff aides in relation to their access to policy makers, their prestige, and the departmental resources available to them. Thus, they act in a manner designed not to jeopardize their position. Again we see that decisions concerning policy formulation are more closely related to bureaucratic and political considerations than they are to scientific judgments concerning the quality or objectivity of the available information.

The Importance of Information Policy. All information collected by an agency has its place in the agency's general policy. Information is not collected simply because it may prove interesting. New information is integrated into the agency's overall information-gathering needs. In transmitting information, staff members rely primarily upon their experience and expertise as they judge whether to transmit a piece of information and what portions of the information to send on. Full reports are rarely sent through the decision-making channels. These propositions can be reformulated in the following manner: The transmission of information is dependent upon the tradition of expertise in a given policy area. This study has provided some evidence that policy makers value the expertise of their trusted aides more than any other source of information. More investigation is needed before one could reach a definitive conclusion.

Established bureaucratic rules and procedures do limit the use of information. Information generated in-house and other social science information tended to be used more by respondents than the CNS information was, except in the energy policy areas. However, it is important to note that the energy policy makers and staffs were most guilty of not making appropriate use of the survey instrument. The importance of bureaucratic rules and procedures also helps to explain why the CNS information was used less than the other two kinds. In addition, we found that the multiagency nature of the project helped to contribute to the saliency of organizational factors. The problems of coordination and competition over control of information resources highlight these organizational concerns. Agencies would not have written new RFPs for the purpose of receiving a continuous national survey administered through one agency alone if this were not the case.

The CNS experiment does not represent a unique, special, or peculiar experience relative to information processing within federal bureaucracies, as a whole. If anything, the use made of this information was greater and more intense than that of information normally contracted for by our agency participants. The interviews show that the criteria used to judge these data, the decision-making process used to evaluate NORC's services, and the criteria for selectivity were not unique to this particular project. Indeed, the respondents contended that survey research information is not treated in a manner different than other information resources generated by external contractors.

Politics and Utilization

The results of this study underscore the importance of understanding organizational routines and procedures and their influence on the dissemination and use of information in public organizations. In emphasizing this aspect of political behavior, one may be overlooking the traditionally political functions of knowledge: knowledge for the purpose of validating the core values of elected officials. Gamson (1968) and others have conceived of the political function of information utilization as related to the rejection of information that is not ideologically acceptable.

We found no evidence that participants consciously distorted the CNS information. The meaning of the results was not altered by the process of selecting what information to pass on. Analysts might feel that the most important findings were ignored, but the results passed on were not tampered with so as to change their original meaning. During the first wave of utilization, information was not passed on in eleven policy areas; nontransmission was especially high in the nonenergy policy areas. As we have seen, organizational considerations influenced selectivity more than any other factor. This result, by itself, does not lead to the conclusion that information was consciously suppressed. Such a conclusion would imply that staff members knew how policy makers would respond to a piece of information and decided to withhold it in order to avoid a policy decision unfavorable to them. Rather, the participants were concerned with becoming trusted staff aides. Trusted aides do not pass on information if they are unable to calculate the risks involved if the policy maker decides to use it. Within this context, *risks* refers to challenges to overall rewards, budget allocations, and staff resources. These concerns have to do with the allocation of organizational resources, not the formulation of substantive policies. Moreover, this study could not document instances in which research was deliberately misused to serve purely political ends.

Although the study focused on political organizations, the data point to the conclusion that the detected practices and procedures of information processing may also apply to large complex organizations that are not political in character.

The Continuous National Survey experiment, in sum, illustrates that the relationship between government and research institutions is still an "uneasy partnership," to use Lyons' (1969) phrase. Social scientists have long disagreed about the degree to which the social sciences should focus on the pragmatic problems of government. Our research results suggest that if one decides to focus on particular problems in government, one must then negotiate the maze of bureaucratic procedures that govern how information is produced, disseminated, and used.

Questionnaires

Questions for Agencies

1. How would you characterize the genesis of this project— what sticks out most in your mind?
2. Why were you (your agency) interested in this project?
3. What did you hope the project would do for your agency— what impact was it to have? Has it been successful in meeting your initial expectations? Similarly, did you have hopes of what it would do for you?
4. What information specifically did you hope the project would provide for your agency? How was this to be integrated with other information that is being collected by the agency?
5. What are these other types (kinds) of information which are being collected?
6. How would you characterize your initial contacts with

RANN concerning this project? What contact have you had with RANN since that time?

7. Were you the only one in your agency interested in this project or were there others also interested? Who were these other people? Did they stay in touch with you concerning the progress of your work with the project? Did this change over time?

8. How would you characterize your initial meeting with representatives of NORC? Were they responsive to your ideas? Did you find them easy to work with? Did this change at all over time? (If they weren't flexible, why did this seem to be the case?)

9. Were the goals of the project clear to you from the beginning? Did they seem to be consonant with goals you were also pursuing? If not, how did your goals differ from theirs?

10. When you suggested something, were you satisfied that it was incorporated into the questionnaires being prepared?

11. Did you have any questions about the sampling techniques proposed or were these O.K. with you?

12. How did the communications patterns work with NORC? Did you suggest ideas to them, which were then developed by NORC, or did they suggest ideas to you, or just how did it work?

13. What sort of scheduling was set up for delivery of processed information? Were you satisfied with this schedule in terms of the time constraints you were under? If not, why not?

14. Did NORC seem flexible with respect to these time schedules?

15. How would you characterize your meetings with OMB on this project? Was NORC helpful in securing clearance?

16. What was your initial reaction when you learned that you were no longer going to receive this service as part of a grant?

17. Who was consulted in making the decision to provide agency funds to continue with this project?

18. On what basis was this decision made?

19. Did you find the survey research instrument useful for the

kinds of problems you needed to solve at the time the service was available to you? What are the pros and cons involved here?

20. Over the period of the time that the project has been in existence, what do you perceive the biggest problems to have been? What were the biggest assets with respect to your agency?

21. Were you specifically assigned to work with NORC? What instructions were you given at the time you were assigned to the project?

22. If you had any complaints during the course of the development of the project, whom did you feel you could communicate them to?

23. Ideally, what would you like your relationship with NORC or an agency like NORC to be?

24. Do you feel that this project has been a success? Why yes or why no (as detailed an answer as possible)?

25. In general, what do you feel is the usefulness of social science data for federal agencies and public policy decisions in general? Has your experience with this project altered your impressions at all?

26. Has your relationship with RANN continued to be a good one? Why or why not?

Questions for RANN and NSF

1. How would you characterize the genesis of this project: What sticks out most in your mind?

2. Why was and is RANN interested in this particular area?

3. How would you characterize your initial meetings with representatives of NORC? What were their responses to your ideas?

4. Given that you felt negatively about the first few drafts that NORC submitted, what was it specifically that you were looking for that was not there?

5. In the end, what were the major reasons for funding the project?

6. Were you satisfied that the inputs you suggested (as differentiated from stipulations for funding) were incorporated into the proposal? If not, what was left out that you felt was important?

7. What did you like and dislike about what NORC suggested?

8. How do you evaluate the target populations NORC was surveying?

9. Why was the project funded for only one year instead of the three originally requested?

10. Once the project was funded, how would you characterize your relations with NORC? Were there any specific problems? If yes, what were they? Please consider this question in the context of four specific time periods: June-August 1972, September-December 1972, January-October 1973, November 1973 until now.

11. Was there any one person who was particularly helpful at NORC?

12. On what basis was it decided which agencies would participate in the project and which would not? How did you make contact with these agencies—by letter, meetings, or what?

13. How would you characterize the response of the various agencies you contacted concerning this project?

14. In your initial contacts with the agencies, what substantive details concerning the project did you pass on to them?
    a. Did you suggest anything to them about how they might use the surveys?
    b. Did they ask questions about the uses of the survey or any questions of this sort?

15. Within a given agency, who did you make contact with (what position were they in)? Is this the person you wanted to make contact with? Were you hoping to gain contact with a specific type of people (policy people, assistant directors, or what)?

16. Why did you choose to make contact with Mr. or Ms. X within a given agency?

17. How would you characterize your relations with the agencies originally involved with the project?

18. During the course of this project, what contact did you have with the agencies? What contact did you have with OMB? Did the pattern of frequency of these contacts change over time?

19. Did the agencies ever contact you with any evaluative comments concerning this project? If yes, how did you respond to these agencies?

20. What do you feel was your appropriate role with respect to these agencies throughout the project?

21. It is my understanding that you were to have a place on the questionnaire for all of the cycles. What use did you make of this? What was the basis of your decision to use it or not use it?

22. How would you characterize your attitude when you learned that NORC would not have sufficient funds to carry on the project for all the cycles of questionnaires that were originally planned?

23. When it became clear that the agencies would have to provide their own funds if they wanted to continue as clients of NORC, what did you feel the appropriate role of RANN to be: Was it one of trying to help NORC, or trying to remain completely independent of NORC, or what?

24. Given this project, by what criteria can one or should one judge the success or failure of the project? Or shouldn't one be talking in these terms at all?

25. In your opinion, has the project been a success? Why yes, why no?

26. In your mind, what were the biggest problems this project faced up until now? Have NORC and the agencies responded effectively to these problems?

27. In general, what do you feel is the usefulness of social science data for federal agencies and public policy decisions in general? Has the experience of this project altered your impressions at all?

28. Why did you make the decision not to grant extra funds to this project? Let me refer to four specific cases.

    a. Extra 10 percent talked about during the summer of 1973

b. September-October 1973, when extra funding was once again discussed

c. Concerning research on the present energy situation

d. In June, when CNS was about to go out of the field

29. In general, what does RANN see as the pay-offs from its projects?

30. More specifically, what criteria does RANN use for funding projects in general?

31. Given the context of the last two questions, how does the CNS fit into your goals and hopeful outputs?; that is, what does RANN see as its mission?

Questions for OMB

1. When did you first learn of this project? Who contacted you?

2. What was your initial reaction when you heard about the details of the project?

3. Did your impressions of the project change over time? Why?

4. How would you characterize your initial meetings with members of NORC and the various agencies involved?

5. What were the problems in granting clearance? How were these initial problems met? Did there continue to be any problems after that point? What was the nature of those problems?

6. Ideally, how do you feel that the agencies could best make use of the service that is being offered to them? Which agencies have made best use of it, which ones haven't? Why do you feel some have and some haven't?

7. Do you feel that NORC has been helpful in guiding agencies in making best use of this service?

8. How can this information best be integrated with other information that agencies are collecting? What is the nature of these other types of information?

9. Do you feel that this project offered information which could be used for policy purposes? Was it so used?

10. How would you characterize your relations with NORC over time?

11. Did you continue to have contact with RANN after the initiation of the project? If yes, how would you characterize this contact?

12. What are the special problems involved with granting clearance? Are there special problems involved with this type (kind) of information?

13. When you learned that the RANN funds were running out for this project, what did you feel your appropriate role to be? Was it one of encouraging the agencies to continue or what?

14. On what basis did you make your decision of what to do and what not to do?

15. It is my understanding that you had a place on the questionnaire. How did you decide how to make use of this space? Did your needs change over time? Did you find NORC responsive to your needs?

16. As it became clear that NORC needed more funds, did you encourage NORC staff to continue their projects?

17. Did you suggest any strategy to them on how they might gain more funds?

18. In general, do you feel that the project has been a success?

19. In general, what do you feel is the usefulness of social science data for federal agencies and public policy? Has the experience of this project altered your impressions at all?

Questions for Agencies (Spring 1974, Spring 1975)

1. What contact have you had with the CNS since it went out of the field?

2. Now that you have received most of the reports from NORC, could you go through policy area by policy area and tell me what use, if any, this information was put to?

3. How do you account for this?

4. What level of policy was this information aimed at? How does this differ from question area to question area?

5. Could you also tell me something about the flow of information: When the NORC reports were received, what happened to them? Who was informed of the results?
6. How did you go about selecting what information to send?
7. Is there anything special you would point to concerning how this information resource was used within your agency?
8. Similarly, is there anything special you would point to concerning the relations between NORC and your agency?
9. As you remember, one of the goals of the CNS experiment was to provide policy makers with policy-relevant information. To what extent was this done? How do you account for this?
10. What might have been done to get policy makers more involved or interested in the project?
11. Looking back at the policy areas to which the CNS information was applied, what other kinds of information were applied to the same areas? I am particularly interested in:
   a. Other kinds of social science related information
   b. In-house generated information
   c. Newspaper and popular journals
   For each resource, was it put to greater, equal, or less use than the CNS information and why?
12. Given the policy needs of your agency, what, if anything, could have been done to make the CNS information more useful?
13. What constraints were put on the utilization of the CNS information? Were these peculiar to the CNS? How do they differ for other kinds of information resources?
14. When information is utilized for policy purposes within your agency, what factors are critical in understanding why it is or isn't utilized by policy makers? Let me mention a few factors, and I would like you to tell me whether they are of great importance, some importance, or no importance at all.
   a. "The information supports the policy position the decision makers are predisposed toward."
   b. "The information comes directly to the decision maker through a trusted staff aide."

    c. "It has not moved up through the decision-making hierarchy but come in laterally."

    d. The information was produced in-house as opposed to being provided by an outside contractor.

    e. It is on a timely topic of interest and need.

    f. It is a unique source of information.

    g. The objectivity of the producer is unquestionable.

    h. It is written in a manner that is understandable.

    i. It does not challenge or contradict a position already taken by a decision maker.

    j. It does not challenge the budget or staff allocations of the agency.

15. If you had to pick one or two of these factors that were most important for understanding utilization, what would they be?

16. Do these factors apply to the utilization of the CNS information?

17. Would you like to see the CNS in the field right now? If yes, how would you use it or something like it?

18. In retrospect, to what extent would you say that the CNS was a success?

19. In this context, is there anything you would point to of particular importance?

20. If you had to do it over again, what would you change?

21. In retrospect, how could the coordination problem have been changed?

22. As you remember, one of the goals for this project was to develop information that could be used in the construction of social indicators. To what extent was this done?

23. Would you have liked to have seen it done?

24. At any time in this experiment, was there an agency view or decision on this project that was different from your own? What criteria were used to formulate the agency's view?

Basic Coding Sheet
and Summary Tables

Table B1. Basic Coding Sheet

Stage 1 (Initial Contact)	*Stage 2* (Development of Questions)	*Stage 3* (Decision to Continue or Not)	*Stage 4* (Present Status)
Contact 1 (Place in hierarchy) Contact 2 (Place in hierarchy) Contact 3 (Place in hierarchy)	Contacts (same coding as stage 1)	Contacts (same coding as stage 1)	Contacts (same coding as stage 1)
Frequency of contact: Types (for each contact) 1. Each time in Washington 2. Most of the time 3. Only when some results had arrived 4. Once or twice 5. Not at all	Frequency of contact (same coding as stage 1)	Frequency of contact (same coding as stage 1)	Frequency of contact (same coding as stage 1)
Type of participation: 1. Get-acquainted meeting— no substantive discussion. Assign staff person to work with project. 2. Discuss questions to be asked—tell NORC to go write them. 3. Discuss questions—ask	Type of participation: 1. No meetings or no contact. 2. One meeting to discuss NORC results. 3. Discuss NORC report, ask for revisions. 4. Received report(s)—submit revisions to NORC. 5. Write in-house memos, no	Type of participation: 1. No meetings or no contact. 2. One meeting with NORC to discuss agency's experience. 3. Multiple meetings with NORC to discuss agency's experiences. 4. Ask NORC for a proposal— no meeting.	Type of participation: 1. No meetings or no contact. 2. Single exploratory meeting. 3. Multiple meetings. 4. In-house memos, no meetings with NORC. 5. In-house meetings about the project.

(continued on next page)

Table B1 (*Continued*)

Stage 1 (Initial Contact)	Stage 2 (Development of Questions)	Stage 3 (Decision to Continue or Not)	Stage 4 (Present Status)
NORC to work with staff member.	discussion with NORC.	5. Submit written evaluation to NORC.	6. Broker responsible for co-ordination.
4. Discuss questions, write own draft—send to NORC to use.	6. Broker responsible for co-ordination.	6. Write in-house memos, no discussion—no reports to NORC.	7. Meet once or twice outside Washington.
5. Write in-house memos; no further discussion with NORC.	7. Discuss results each time NORC comes to Washington.	7. Broker responsible for co-ordination.	
6. Broker responsible for co-ordination.			
7. No contact.			

Note: Interviewers were to code as many catgories as appropriate.

Table B2. Diversification, Frequency of Contact, Quality of Contacts

	Stage 1	Stage 2	Stage 3	Stage 4
		Agency 1		
Contacts	1. Special assistant to secretary 2. Program administrator 3. Research staff (2)	1. Special assistant to secretary 2. Program administrator 3. Research staff (2) 4. Assistant secretary (2) 5. Secretary	1. Special assistant to secretary 4. Assistant secretary (2) 5. Secretary	1. Special assistant to secretary 4. Assistant secretary (2) 5. Secretary
Frequency	Type 1 for Contact 1 Type 5 for Contact 2 Type 4 for Contact 3	Type 1/Contact 1 Type 3/Contact 2 Type 3/Contact 3 Type 4/Contact 4 Type 5/Contact 5	Type 1/Contact 1 Type 4/Contact 4 Type 4/Contact 5	Type 3/Contact 1 Type 5/Contact 2 Type 5/Contact 3 Type 5/Contact 4 Type 5/Contact 5
Type of participation	Types 4 and 6/Contact 1 Types 1 and 6/Contact 2 Types 1 and 6/Contact 3	Types 6 and 7/Contact 1 Type 2/Contact 2 Type 2/Contact 3 Types 1 and 6/Contact 4 Types 1 and 6/Contact 5	Type 3/Contact 1 Types 2 and 7/Contact 4 Types 2 and 7/Contact 5	Type 7/Contact 1 Type 1/rest of the contacts
		Agency 2		
Contacts	1. Research staff	1. Research staff 2. Research staff (2) 3. Division boss 4. Assistant secretary	1. Research staff 2. Research staff (2) 3. Division boss 4. Assistant secretary	1. Research staff 2. Research staff (2)

(continued on next page)

Table B2 *(Continued)*

	Stage 1	*Stage 2*	*Stage 3*	*Stage 4*
		Agency 2 (Continued)		
Frequency	Type 1/Contact 1	Type 1/Contact 1 Type 2/Contact 2 Type 4/Contact 3 Type 5/Contact 4	Type 1/Contact 1 Type 3/Contact 2 Type 5/Contact 3 Type 5/Contact 4	Type 3/Contact 1 Type 5/Contact 2 Type 5/Contact 3 Type 5/Contact 4
Type of participation	Types 4 and 6/Contact 1	Types 6 and 7/Contact 1 Types 2, 3, and 6/Contact 2 Type 2/Contact 3 Type 1/Contact 4	Types 3-7/Contact 1 Types 1 and 7/rest of contacts	Types 1 and 3/Contact 1 Types 1 and 6/rest of contacts
		Agency 3		
Contacts	1. Research officer 2. Special assistant 3. Program administrator 4. Program administrator	1. Research officer 2. Special assistant 3. Program administrator 4. Program administrator 5. Assistant secretary (2) 6. Secretary 7. Division boss (research)	1. Research officer 2. Special assistant 5. Assistant secretary (2) 6. Secretary 7. Division boss (research)	
Frequency	Type 1/Contacts 1 and 2 Type 2/Contact 3 Type 4/Contact 4	Type 1/Contact 1 Type 3/Contacts 2 and 3 Type 5/Contacts 4-7	Type 2/Contact 1 Type 4/Contact 2 Type 1/rest of contacts	Type 5/all contacts

Type of par- ticipation	Types 3 and 6/Contact 1 Type 2/Contacts 2, 3, and 4	Types 6 and 7/Contact 1 Type 3/Contact 2 Type 2/Contact 3 Type 1/rest of contacts	Types 3 and 7/Contact 1 Type 2 /Contact 2 Type 1/rest of contacts	Type 1/all contacts
		Agency 4		
Contacts	1. Research staff 2. Division boss 3. Assistant secretary, special assistant	1. Research staff 2. Division boss 3. Assistant secretary, special assistant 4. Other research staff (2)	1. Research staff 2. Division boss 3. Assistant secretary, special assistant 4. Other research staff (2) 5. Special assistant to the special assistant 6. Assistant secretary	1. Research staff 2. Division boss 3. Assistant secretary, special assistant 5. Special assistant to the special assistant
Frequency	Type 1/Contact 1 Type 2/Contact 2 Type 5/Contact 3	Type 1/Contact 1 Type 4/Contacts 2, 3, and 4	Type 2/Contact 1 Type 5/Contacts 2, 4, and 6 Type 4/Contacts 3 and 5	Type 4/Contact 1 Type 5/rest of contacts
Type of par- ticipation	Types 4 and 5/Contact 1 Type 7/Contacts 2 and 3	Types 6 and 7/Contact 1 Type 1/Contacts 2 and 4 Type 2/Contact 3	Types 3 and 7/Contact 1 Type 6/Contacts 2, 5, and 6 Type 1/Contact 4	Types 6 and 7/Contact 1 Type 1/rest of contacts

(continued on next page)

Table B2 (*Continued*)

	Stage 1	Stage 2	Stage 3	Stage 4
		Agency 5		
Contacts	Not involved	Became involved at end of this stage 1. Research staff (3) 2. Division boss 3. Other division boss	1. Research staff (3) 2. Division boss 4. Assistant secretary (2) 5. Secretary 6. Research staff (2)	1. Research staff (3) 2. Division boss 4. Assistant secretary (2) 6. Research staff (2)
Frequency		1. Type 1/Contact 1 2. Type 2/Contact 2 3. Type 4/Contact 3	1. Type 2/Contacts 1 and 2 2. Type 5/Contacts 3-5	Type 5/all contacts
Type of participation		1. Types 6 and 7/Contacts 1, 2, and 3	1. Types 3 and 7/Contacts 1, 2, and 6 2. Type 6/Contacts 3 and 5 3. Type 2/Contact 4	Type 5/all contacts
		Agency 7		
Contacts	1. Research staff (2)	1. Research staff (2) 2. Research staff 3. Assistant secretary	1. Research staff (2) 2. Research staff 3. Assistant secretary	1. Research staff (2) 2. Research staff

Frequency	1. Type 1/Contact 1	Type 1/Contact 1 Type 2/Contact 2 Type 5/Contact 3	Type 1/Contact 1 Type 5/Contacts 2 and 3	Type 5/all contacts
Type of participation	1. Type 4/Contact 1	Type 7/Contacts 1 and 2 Type 1/Contact 3	Type 3/Contact 1 Type 6/Contact 3 Type 1/Contact 2	Type 1/all contacts

Agency 6

Contacts	Not involved	1. Program administrator (2) 2. Research staff (2) 3. Research staff	1. Program administrator (2) 2. Research staff (2) 3. Research staff	
Frequency		1. Type 2/Contact 1 2. Type 1/Contacts 2 and 3	Type 4/Contacts 1 and 2 Type 2/Contact 3 Type 5/Contact 4	Type 5/all contacts
Type of participation		Type 7/all contacts	Type 2/Contact 1 Type 6/Contacts 2 and 4 Type 2/Contact 3	Type 1/all contacts

Note: Frequency and type of participation are coded by the scheme presented in Table B1.

Agency Memos, I

▭o▭━━━▭o▭o▭━━━▭o▭

The Questionnaire

The questionnaire which will be administered to the sample respondents is intended to take seventy minutes and will be composed of two major sections. The first section is referred to as the *basic questionnaire*. The responsibility for the design of this section rests with the staff of the National Opinion Research Center. This section of the questionnaire accounts for approximately one half, or thirty-five minutes, of the complete interview schedule. The second section is referred to as the *client questionnaire*. The responsibility for the design of this section rests with the federal agencies serving as users. Since there are multiple users, the remaining thirty-five minutes of the interview time is equally divided among the major agencies with each having responsibilityfor its own subsection. Each agency works closely with the staff of NORC in both the design and item construction of each section.

182

The Basic Questionnaire

This section of the complete interview schedule is intended to remain essentially unchanged throughout the first year of data collection. It has three distinct purposes. First, to collect from each respondent basic background or demographic information normally used in tabulations of survey results. Second, to collect subjective information, for example, attitudes or perceptions, concerning selected aspects of neighborhood and community life with a special emphasis on local service systems. Third, to collect information which is needed for the analysis of the subjective data on service systems.

The summary description of the questionnaire items contains eleven subsections, each of which includes item labels and numbers which can be used to refer to the draft questionnaire items. These eleven subsections can be arranged according to the three purposes mentioned above.

Purpose	*Subsection*
Background	I
Neighborhood and Service	III, VI, VIII, IX, X
Analytic and Control	II, IV, V, VII, XI

The following discussion elaborates on each subsection.

Subsection I—Background. These questions are asked in traditional formats consistent with standard data sources, such as the census, and with NORC's experience. These items provide the information necessary to: (1) evaluate other item responses in terms of socioeconomic status indicators; (2) relate responses on other items to the general population by standardization of these items; and (3) construct indicators for use in analyses of other items, such as prestige, position in the life cycle, and the like.

Subsection II—Affective Data. These items are taken from Bradburn's study *The Structure of Psychological Well Being* (Chicago: Aldine, 1959) and Bradburn and Sudman's study reported in *Racial Integration in American Neighborhoods* (Chicago: Aldine, 1970). These items are of interest for the following reasons: (1) Measures of happiness and affect-balance can be used to adjust the various satisfaction measures for individual differences in general mood; (2) Affect measures can serve as a global quality-of-life or experience indicator which may vary significantly over neighborhoods; (3) Seasonal variation in mood may be significant and therefore of possible relevance to the unique time-sequence design of this survey; and (4) Racial attitudes are potential determinants of reactions to the neighborhood as well as actions, such as those measured in the participation items.

Subsection III—Satisfactions. These items are intended to furnish information relevant to the net subjective impact of various personal and local conditions. They provide quality-of-life indicators which can in fact be related to other kinds of data collected in the questionnaire, as the following examples show.

Satisfaction with:	*Other Directly Relevant Information:*
Financial situation	Family income (I.1)
Dwelling unit	Dwelling unit measures (V)
Neighborhood	(a) Neighborhood characteristics (VI, X)
	(b) Local services (VIII, IX)
Job	Occupation (I.6-10)
Grocery store	Store characteristics (VIII.3-7)
Clinics and health centers	Clinic characteristics (VIII.1)
Doctors	Doctor characteristics (VIII.2)
Police	Police characteristics (VIII.8)
Transportation	Mode and purpose characteristics (IX)
Life	Other satisfactions

Subsection IV—Community and Government Participation and Perception. These items provide information which can serve to aid in interpreting the social importance of the satisfaction measures. It seems reasonable to assume that areas in which satisfactions are low and in which participation is relatively high will, over time, increase their level of satisfaction. In particular, the level of local self-help efforts can be related both to perceptions and to attitudes concerning local events. Evaluation of such possible interdependencies, especially at the neighborhood level and over time, can provide useful policy data regarding programmatic alternatives relevant to the subjective dimensions of effectiveness.

Subsection V—Dwelling Unit. Most of these questions replicate those used in the 1970 census. They provide useful information at the household level (for example, as explanatory variables for various individual subjective measures) as well as at the aggregate neighborhood level (for example, as neighborhood quality indicators).

Subsection VI—Neighborhood. These items are taken from previous studies of migration behavior. They can be used to assess the five-to-ten-year national changes in the distribution of preferred characteristics. They can also be used to provide data relevant to issues of population distribution in relation to selected local characteristics desired by residents. In addition, neighborhood and community tenure data are useful in interpreting other item responses regarding subjective reactions to local events.

Subsection VII—Migration. These items have also been taken from past migration studies. The information on last move is of interest in comparison to data obtained five and ten years ago with this item. Also, it is helpful in interpreting the significance of the reactions to the present neighborhood on future moves. It is also possible to explore the geographical clustering of respondents in terms of their motivation for a recent residential shift. It may be that characteristics of the present residence are related to reasons for migration, thus enabling heuristic projections of residential shifts.

Subsections VIII and IX—Local Services and Transportation. These items explore multiple aspects of local services relevant to the quality of life in most areas. In addition to the explanation of satisfaction measures, it is useful to evaluate the geographical clustering of service characteristics over services and possibly to develop an index of neighborhood service quality. Also, aggregation of data to the neighborhood level over time and respondents provides data useful in exploring the possible dynamic interdependence of service characteristics. These data provide a generally richer source of information than that previously available concerning the subjective side of public and private services on the local level.

   Subsection X—Victimization. The items have been taken from the ongoing survey conducted by the Law Enforcement Assistance Administration. It is hoped that these data, both on the individual and aggregated neighborhood level, can be used to assess the impact of personally experienced crime on subjective reactions to the neighborhood and to assess changes over time in incidence rates nationally and at lower aggregation levels.

   Subsection XII—Health. These items are taken from the periodic household survey conducted by the National Center for Health Statistics. They will be used in the analysis of the health care items and in constructing neighborhood quality indicators if significant between-neighborhood variability is found.

The Sample

   This survey will be based on a national probability sample of the adult, eighteen years of age and over, noninstitutionalized population. The general sampling design is described in the enclosed document authored by B. King and C. Richards. This design will be revised according to procedures not yet documented. These procedures will preserve the full probability character of the sample over time.

   The time-sequence design of the survey has been developed in order to allow the analyst the flexibility to aggregate information over population units (neighborhoods, population survey units, metropolitan areas) or time units (months, quarters).

Agency Memos, II

━◘━━━◘━◘━━━◘━

**The Potential Impact of Extended Daylight Saving Time
Policies on Energy Conservation in the U.S.**

The RAND Corporation proposes to conduct a study of the
benefits and disbenefits of extending daylight saving time (DST)
through such measures as: (1) winter DST (resulting in one hour
of daylight saving all year round); or (2) one hour of DST in fall
and winter and two hours in spring and summer (double DST).
The objective of the study will be to identify, among the spec-
trum of possibilities, the most promising extended DST policies
and to estimate the energy savings that would be expected to result from implementing such policies.

Certain energy effects of extending DST appear to be
tractable to analysis. Specifically, these include the energy used
for electric lighting in the residential sector and certain parts of
the commercial sector, and the energy used for heating and

cooling residential buildings and certain classes of commercial buildings. These will be evaluated through use of a technique employing annual sunrise-sunset patterns and annual temperature patterns for specific urban locations in the U.S. Computerized simulation models of buildings will also be used for quantitatively estimating the energy effects of various DST schedules.

Evaluating the effects of extended DST on fuel consumption in transportation modes appears to be tractable by employing interaction terms (on constants and variables) in a multiple-regression equation of fuel consumption. In addition, certain other approaches for assaying the consumption of gasoline in automobiles under various DST policies are proposed. These methods depend on finding correlations between seasonal gasoline consumption and DST policies in states that had different DST observances at the same times in the past.

Attitudes about the extension of DST that are held by people from different walks of life will be evaluated during the study. Data already collected by the National Research Opinion Council on winter DST will be used as the basis of this evaluation.

Analytical Methods: Energy Effects

Lighting. Daylight saving measures could result in savings in electric lighting in sectors of the economy where it is possible to substitute natural daylight for artificial illumination. This may be illustrated by Figure 1 [not reproduced here] which shows annual sunrise-sunset patterns, with standard time of day on one axis and day of year on the other, for Los Angeles and San Francisco. Superimposed on the display are assumed times of waking up and going to bed for a typical residential household. The assumed schedule is: arise at 6:30 A.M. and retire by 10:30 P.M. by the clock. The impacts of various DST measures can readily be compared by measuring areas on such displays, taking regional patterns into consideration. From this display it is apparent that the present one-hour summer DST policy (last Sunday in April to last Sunday in October) results in the saving of electricity for illumination (relative to standard time year-round) mainly by getting people to bed earlier. It is also evident that additional savings of illumination electricity could be made (under the above assumption) by beginning DST earlier in the year, by continuing it longer, and by having double daylight saving (two hours) during the middle months of the year. The nighttime waking hours when artificial illumination is needed in the residential sector are indicated, for L.A., by the stippled area in Figure 1.

This technique will be used to evaluate the effects of DST on residential illumination and, if feasible, on illumination in those parts of the commercial and industrial sectors that can make use of natural sunlight, such businesses as garages, service stations, outdoor parking lots, and some recreational and amusement facilities. On the other hand, there are many commercial enterprises in which the level of illumination would not be expected to be affected by DST. These are businesses in which the interior illumination is independent of outside conditions of daylight or darkness. Quantitative estimates will be made of energy savings for electric lighting in all affected sectors.

Heating and Cooling. Patterns of heating and cooling of buildings would be affected by the various DST measures. This could result in significant energy savings. Two different analytical methods will be used in conjunction to provide quantitative estimates of DST effects on energy use for heating and cooling buildings, particularly in the commercial and residential sectors. The first method is to use simulation models of buildings, such as E-CUBE [. . .].

Survey of Past Experience and Prior Studies

Experience with year-round daylight saving time during World War II in Great Britain (1941-1944) and the United States (1942-1945) suggests that net energy savings might be realized by extending the use of daylight saving time. Various measures to extend daylight saving time (DST) can readily be envisioned. Examples are: one hour of DST all year round, instead of only the six months from April to October as at present; one hour of DST in fall and winter and two hours of DST in spring and summer; also the dates beginning and ending the transitions could be changed. Among the various conceivable alternatives, there is undoubtedly one that has the greatest potential for conserving energy on the national level.

Information on the impact of past experiences with DST will be examined with the objectives of quantifying possible energy savings from past DST programs and identifying other significant nonenergy effects. Prior studies will be surveyed to consolidate their results, to ensure that any indicated energy savings are expressed on a common basis (such as percentage of total national energy consumption) and to interpret their findings in the light of the changes that have taken place in the interim so that results may be updated. Prior studies on DST that will be evaluated will include among others: the Bary report of 1943, and the AEIC report of 1947, both of which focus on electricity savings during WW II; the California PUC report of 1949, which estimated the electricity savings in California from extending DST because of a hydroelectric shortage; the 1970 Federal Power Commission survey of electric utility companies' estimates of fuel savings from year-round DST; and British reports on the effects of year-round DST on automobile driving habits and traffic accidents.

Additional insights may be obtainable from statistical data from Indiana, which has had year-round DST (1964-1966), summer DST only (1967-1970), and year-round standard time (1971). Data on electricity, natural gas, heating oil, and gasoline consumption in Indiana during these years will be examined to see whether any DST effects can be discerned. On the national level as well as on the individual state levels, these types of data will be examined at the time periods immediately before and after the beginning of DST in the spring and the end of DST in the fall. It is already evident that less electricity is used in the last week of DST in the fall than in the first week after return to standard time. For this particular time period the average reduction in electricity consumption nationwide attributable to DST amounts to about 1.8 percent. The savings ascribable to DST at the spring changeover are considerably less, about 0.2

percent. If the observed savings can be correlated with prevailing temperature conditions or other natural phenomena, it may be possible to make useful inferences permitting the results to be applied to other periods of time as well.

References

Aaron, H. J. *Politics and the Professions.* Washington, D.C.: The Brookings Institution, 1978.

Arrow, K. J. *The Limits of Organization.* New York: Norton, 1974.

Barker, E. *The Development of Public Services in Europe.* New York: Oxford University Press, 1944.

Bell, D. *The Coming of Post-Industrial Society.* New York: Basic Books, 1974.

Bendix, R. *Max Weber: An Intellectual Portrait.* New York: Doubleday Anchor Books, 1962.

Blau, P. *The Dynamics of Bureaucracy.* Chicago: University of Chicago Press, 1955.

Blau, P., and Meyer, M. *Bureaucracy in Modern Society.* New York: Random House, 1971.

Campbell, D. T. "Reforms as Experiments." *American Psychologist,* 1969, *24* (4), 409-428.

Campbell, D. T. "Administrative Experiments, Institutional Records, and Non-Reactive Measures." In W. Evans (Ed.), *Organizational Experiments.* New York: Harper & Row, 1971a.

Campbell, D. T. "Methods for the Experimenting Society." Manuscript presented at meetings of the Eastern Psychological Association, Washington, D.C., April 1971b.

Caplan, N. S. "The Minimum Conditions Necessary for Utilization." In C. Weiss (Ed.), *Uses of Social Research in Public Policy Making.* Lexington, Mass.: Heath, 1977.

Caplan, N. S. "The Two-Community Theory and Knowledge Utilization." *American Behavioral Scientist,* 1979, *22,* 459-470.

Caplan, N. S. "The State of the Art: What We Know About Utilization." In L. A. Braskamp and R. D. Brown (Eds.), *New Directions for Program Evaluation: Utilization of Evaluative Information,* no. 5. San Francisco: Jossey-Bass, 1980.

Caplan, N. S., and Rich, R. F. "Open and Closed Knowledge-Inquiry Systems: The Process and Consequences of Bureaucratization of Information Policy at the National Level." Paper presented at meeting of the Organization of Economic and Community Development conference on Dissemination of Economic and Social Development and Research Results, Bogota, Colombia, June 1976.

Caplan, N. S., and others. *The Use of Social Science Knowledge in Policy Decisions at the National Level.* Ann Arbor, Mich.: Institute for Social Research, 1975.

Cassidy, S., and others. "Evaluating an Experimental College Reform with Institutional Records: An Interim Report." Unpublished manuscript, 1965.

Crozier, M. *The Bureaucratic Phenomenon: An Examination of Bureaucracy in Modern Organization and Its Cultural Setting in France.* Chicago: University of Chicago Press, 1964.

Douglas, J. D. *American Social Order.* New York: Free Press, 1971.

Downs, A. *An Economic Theory of Democracy.* New York: Harper & Row, 1957.

Dunn, W. "The Two-Communities Metaphor and Models of Knowledge Use: An Exploratory Case Survey." In *Knowledge: Creation, Diffusion, Utilization*, 1980, *1* (4), 515-537.

Einaudi, L. *Assistance to Peru: A Case Study, 1963-1968*. Santa Monica, Calif.: RAND Corporation, 1974.

Eisenstadt, S. N. *The Political Systems of Empires*. New York: Free Press, 1969.

Eisenstadt, S. N. *Federal Statistics Report of the President's Commission*. Vols. 1 and 2. Washington, D.C.: U.S. Government Printing Office, 1971.

Federal Statistics: A Report of the President's Commission on Federal Statistics. Washington, D.C.: U.S. Government Printing Office, 1971.

Franck, T. M., and Weisband, E. (Eds.). *Secrecy and Foreign Policy*. New York: Oxford University Press, 1974.

Gamson, W. *Power and Discontent*. Chicago: Dorsey Press, 1968.

George, A. L. "The Case for Multiple Advocacy in Making Foreign Policy." *The American Political Science Review*, 1972, *66*, 751-785.

Gordon, A. C., and Campbell, D. T. "Recommended Accountability Guidelines for the Evaluation of Improvements in the Delivery of State Social Services." Unpublished manuscript, Northwestern University, 1971.

Hauser, P. M. "Statistics and Politics." Paper prepared for annual meetings of the American Statistical Association, Washington, D.C., August 1972.

Horowitz, I. L. *The Rise and Fall of Project Camelot: Studies in the Relationship Between Social Science and Practical Politics*. Cambridge, Mass.: M.I.T. Press, 1967.

Horowitz, I. L. (Ed.). *The Use and Abuse of Social Science: Behavioral Science and National Policy Making*. New Brunswick, N.J.: Transaction Books, 1971.

Ikeda, K., Yinger, J. M., and Laycock, F. "Reforms as Experiments and Experiments as Reforms." Paper delivered at the Ohio Valley Sociological Meetings, Columbus, Ohio, May 1970.

Ikeda, K., Wolfe, J. A., and Rich, R. F. "The Association of Racial Status, Socioeconomic Status, and Measured Ability upon Academic Performance in a Liberal Arts College." Paper delivered at Ohio Valley Sociological Meetings, Cincinnati, May 1971.

Ilchman, W. "Measure for Measure: Administrative Productivity in the Second Development Decade." Paper for panel seminar, Berkeley, Calif., March 1973.

Ilchman, W., and Uphoff, T. *The Political Economy of Change*. Berkeley: University of California Press, 1971.

"The Information Revolution." *The Annals of the American Academy of Political and Social Science*, 1974, *412*.

Kissinger, H. A. *American Foreign Policy*. Vol. 1. New York: Norton, 1969.

Kitsuse, J., and Cicourel, A. V. "A Note on the Use of Official Statistics." *Social Problems*, 1969, (11), 131-139.

"Knowledge into Action: Improving the Nation's Use of the Social Sciences." Report of the Special Commission on the Social Sciences of the National Science Board. Washington, D.C.: National Science Foundation, 1969.

Levine, R. A. *Public Planning: Failure and Redirection*. New York: Basic Books, 1972.

Likert, R. "The Dual Function of Statistics." *Journal of the American Statistical Association*, 1960, *55*, 1-7.

Lynd, R. S. *Knowledge for What?* Princeton, N.J.: Princeton University Press, 1939.

Lyons, G. M. *The Uneasy Partnership*. New York: Russell Sage Foundation, 1969.

Mannheim, K. *Ideology and Utopia*. New York: Harvest Books, 1936.

March, J. G., and Simon, H. A. *Organizations*. New York: Wiley, 1958.

Marshall, T. H. *Class, Citizenship, and Social Development*. New York: Doubleday Anchor Books, 1965.

Merton, R., and others (Eds.). *Reader in Bureaucracy*. New York: Free Press, 1952.

Moynihan, D. P. *Maximum Feasible Misunderstanding*. New York: Free Press, 1969.

Moynihan, D. P. *Coping*. New York: Random House, 1973.

National Academy of Sciences. *The Federal Investment in*

Knowledge of Social Problems. Washington, D.C.: National Academy of Sciences, 1977.

Northwestern Law Review. Summer 1974 (entire issue).

Office of Management and Budget. Internal Study within the Statistical Policy Division, 1976.

Peters, C., and Branch, T. *Blowing the Whistle.* New York: Praeger, 1972.

Popper, K. "On Reason and the Open Society." *Encounter,* 1972, *37* (5), 13-19.

"Public Access to Information: A Research Study." *Northwestern Law Review,* 1973, *68* (2), entire issue.

Reiss, A., Jr. "Monitoring the Quality of the Criminal Justice System." In A. Campbell and P. E. Converse (Eds.), *Human Meaning of Social Change.* New York: Russell Sage Foundation, 1972.

Rheinstein, M., and Shils, E. (Eds.). *Max Weber on Law in Economy and Society.* New York: Simon & Schuster, 1954.

Rich, R. F. "Editor's Introduction." *American Behavioral Scientist,* 1979, *22,* 327-337.

Robertson, L. S., Rich, R. F., and Ross, H. L. "Jail Sentences for Driving While Intoxicated in Chicago: A Judicial Action that Failed." *Law and Society Review,* 1973, *56,* 55-67.

Rose, R. *Social Policies and Social Indicators.* New York: Social Science Research Council, 1973.

Rosenberg, H. *Bureaucracy, Aristocracy, and Autocracy: The Prussian Experience, 1660-1815.* Cambridge, Mass.: Harvard University Press, 1958.

Rosenbloom, D. H. *Federal Service and the Constitution: The Development of the Public Employment Relationship.* Ithaca, N.Y.: Cornell University Press, 1971.

Ross, H. L., Campbell, D. R., and Glass, G. V. "Determining the Social Effects of Legal Reform." *American Behavioral Scientist,* 1970, *13* (4), 493-508.

Rudolph, L. I., and Rudolph, S. H. "Modern and Traditional Administration Reexamined: A Revisionist Interpretation of Weber on Bureaucracy." Paper presented at International Political Science Association, Edinburgh, August 1973.

Sackman, Y., and Nie, N. (Eds.). *The Information Utility and Social Choice.* Montvale, N.J.: AFIPS Press, 1970.

Schelling, T. "On the Ecology of Micromotives." *The Public Interest,* 1971, (25), 59-99.

Schlesinger, A. M., Jr. *The Imperial Presidency.* Boston: Houghton Mifflin, 1973.

Shonfield, A., and Shaw, S. (Eds.). *Social Indicators and Social Policy.* Social Science Research Council, 1972.

Simon, H. A. *Administrative Behavior.* New York: Macmillan, 1947.

Skolnick, J. H. *Justice Without Trial.* New York: Wiley, 1975.

Snow, C. P. *Science and Government.* Harvard University Godkin Lectures. New York: New American Library, 1962.

Storing, H. A. (Ed.). *Essays on the Scientific Study of Politics.* New York: Holt, Rinehart and Winston, 1962.

Use of Social Research in Federal Domestic Programs: A Staff Study for the Research and Technical Programs Subcommittee of the Committee of Government Operations, House of Representatives, April, 1967. Vols. 2 and 3. Washington, D.C.: U.S. Government Printing Office, 1967.

Webb, E., Campbell, D. T., and Sechrest, L. *Unobtrusive Measures.* Chicago: Rand McNally, 1966.

Weber, M. *From Max Weber: Essays in Sociology.* (H. H. Gerth and C. W. Mills, Eds.) New York: Oxford University Press, 1946.

Weber, M. *The Theory of Social and Economic Organization.* (T. Parsons, Ed.) New York: Oxford University Press, 1947.

Weber, M. *Economy and Society.* (G. Roth and C. Wittich, Eds.) New York: Bedminister Press, 1968.

Weiss, C. H. "The Politicization of Evaluation Research." *Journal of Social Issues,* 1970, *26* (4), 57-68.

Weiss, C. H. (Ed.). *Uses of Social Research in Public Policy Making.* Lexington, Mass.: Heath, 1977.

Wheeler, S. *On Record.* New York: Russell Sage Foundation, 1969.

Wilensky, H. I. *Organizational Intelligence.* New York: Basic Books, 1967.

Index

Aaron, H. J., 3
Access to information, by federal agencies. *See* Organizational access to information
Administrative experiments, 1-2
Agency participants. *See* Federal agency participants
Agriculture, U.S. Department of (DOA), 24, 44, 45, 64
Amalgam, Continuous National Survey as, 27

Bell, D., 4
Brim, O., 3, 4
Brim Report, 17-18
Brokers, agency: involvement with project, 160-161; motivations of, 61-62; and project support, 85; and questionnaire formulation, 64; risks of, 85, 160-161; role of, 15-16, 58-59, 77, 105, 106, 159
Bureaucratic rules and procedures: adherence to, 75, 80-81; and coordination problems, 95, 96; flexibility of, 106; importance of, in project, 96, 99, 157; and knowledge-inquiry system, 102-104, 159; priority given to, by policy makers, 160; and use of information, 12-15, 159, 162, 163. *See also* Organizational interests

Campbell, D. T., 154-155
Caplan, N. S., 2, 6, 8, 9, 12, 13, 14, 15, 16, 20, 21, 96-97, 155, 159
Case study, Continuous National Survey as, 20

199